Cambridge Elements

Elements in International Relations
edited by
Jon C. W. Pevehouse
University of Wisconsin–Madison

Tanja A. Börzel
Freie Universität Berlin

Edward D. Mansfield
University of Pennsylvania

Stefanie Walter
University of Zurich

DIGITAL GLOBALIZATION

Politics, Policy, and a Governance Paradox

Stephen Weymouth
Georgetown University

CAMBRIDGE
UNIVERSITY PRESS

Shaftesbury Road, Cambridge CB2 8EA, United Kingdom

One Liberty Plaza, 20th Floor, New York, NY 10006, USA

477 Williamstown Road, Port Melbourne, VIC 3207, Australia

314–321, 3rd Floor, Plot 3, Splendor Forum, Jasola District Centre, New Delhi – 110025, India

103 Penang Road, #05–06/07, Visioncrest Commercial, Singapore 238467

Cambridge University Press is part of Cambridge University Press & Assessment, a department of the University of Cambridge.

We share the University's mission to contribute to society through the pursuit of education, learning and research at the highest international levels of excellence.

www.cambridge.org
Information on this title: www.cambridge.org/9781108978361
DOI: 10.1017/9781108974158

First published 2023

A catalogue record for this publication is available from the British Library.

ISBN 978-1-108-97836-1 Paperback
ISSN 2515-706X (online)
ISSN 2515-7302 (print)

Digital Globalization

Politics, Policy, and a Governance Paradox

Elements in International Relations

DOI: 10.1017/9781108974158
First published online: April 2023

Stephen Weymouth
Georgetown University

Author for correspondence: Stephen Weymouth,
stephen.weymouth@georgetown.edu

Abstract: Digital technologies are reshaping the global economy and complicating cooperation over its governance. Innovations in technology and business propel a new, digitally driven phase of globalization defined by the expansion of cross-border information flows that is provoking political conflict and policy discord. This Element argues that the activities of digital value chains (DVCs), the central economic actors in digital globalization, complicate international economic relations. Digital value chain activities can erode individual privacy, shift tax burdens, and cement monopoly positions. These outcomes generate a new politics of globalization, and governments are responding with increasing restrictions on cross-border data flows. The Element: (1) explains the new sources of political division stemming from digital globalization; (2) documents policy barriers to digital trade; (3) presents a framework to explain digital trade barriers across countries; and (4) assesses the prospects for international cooperation on digital governance, which requires that countries move beyond coordinated liberalization and toward coordinated regulation.

Keywords: artificial intelligence, data localization, data flow restrictions, data privacy, digital economy, digital trade, globalization, international trade, international cooperation

ISBNs: 9781108978361 (PB), 9781108974158 (OC)
ISSNs: 2515-706X (online), 2515-7302 (print)

Contents

1 Introduction

Digital technologies are reshaping the global economy and complicating cooperation over its governance. Novel business models profit from international transfers of data, services, and knowledge (Agrawal et al., 2018a; Baldwin, 2019; Brynjolfsson and McAfee, 2014; Chander, 2013; Cowhey and Aronson, 2017; Manyika et al., 2016; Srivastava, 2021). These innovations in technology and business propel a new, digitally driven phase of globalization defined by the expansion of cross-border information flows that is provoking political conflict and policy discord – the era of digital globalization. Individual countries have pursued different approaches to regulating digital technologies and cross-border data flows. The resulting fragmented digital governance is upending economic integration and cooperation among nations.

Consider the rift between the United States and the European Union (EU) over transatlantic data flows. Transfers of European citizens' personal data to third countries are restricted under Europe's landmark 2018 General Data Protection Regulation (GDPR), a comprehensive data governance act billed by Brussels as "the toughest privacy and security law in the world."[1] To protect the data privacy of EU citizens, the GDPR requires that destination countries conform with EU privacy protections as a prerequisite to personal data transfers. Despite the fact that the United States has no national privacy law, a workaround agreement enabled businesses to transfer customer data from servers in Europe to those in the United States. In 2020, the European Court of Justice struck down this agreement as a violation of the GDPR, casting uncertainty over the future of transatlantic data flows.

Additional digital economy trade frictions include taxes targeting US tech firms, along with billions of dollars in lawsuits filed by EU regulators over what they see as anticompetitive practices by these firms. Despite deep integration in the trade of goods, different regulatory approaches to privacy, taxation, and competition in the United States and Europe – to say nothing of the differences in governance across less cooperative nations – threaten to silo national digital economies.

Why has digital globalization coincided with a decline in international economic cooperation, and what are prospects for the future integration of the digital economy? This Element argues that distinctive features of data-driven business models complicate international economic relations. A politically sustainable digital globalization requires agreements on rules governing the novel forms of economic exchange that digital technologies enable.

---

[1] https://gdpr.eu/what-is-gdpr/

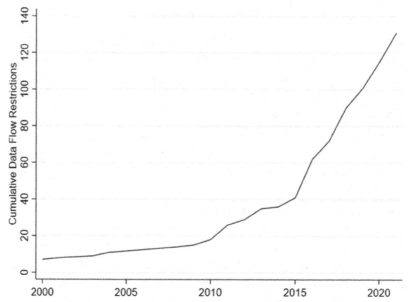

Figure 1 Global cross-border data flow restrictions. Source: Author's calculations based on original dataset (available at https://tinyurl.com/3bx4uyy7)

The argument proceeds in four steps, with a section devoted to each. Section 2 explains how unique characteristics of data, the central factor of production in the digital economy, inflame distrust over the merits of globalization. I highlight the central role of value chains built to monetize cross-border data flows – digital value chains (DVCs) – in new political conflicts and debates. Section 3 documents ways in which governments respond to digital economy concerns with policies that increase the costs of cross-border digital transactions. (As illustrated in Figure 1, impediments to digital trade are sharply increasing.) Section 4 outlines a framework for explaining political support for digital trade restrictions, and assesses the degree to which prevailing models of goods trade restrictions apply to digital services. Section 5 examines the prospects for international cooperation over digital globalization. To overcome sources of resistance and distrust, I contend that countries must coordinate to some degree on regulatory matters beyond the traditional scope of international trade policy.

A central theme of the Element is that digital globalization represents a paradigm shift in international economic governance. In the previous phase of globalization, characterized by goods production and trade, governments lowered trade barriers in order to integrate their economies into global production

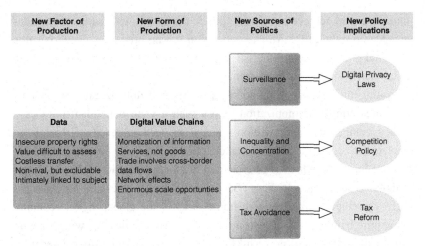

Figure 2 Data, digital value chains, and the new politics of globalization

networks (Baldwin, 2016; Goldstein et al., 2007; Subramanian and Wei, 2007). Integration mainly required coordinated *liberalization* – of tariffs primarily, but also of barriers to international investment. In the current era, coordinated liberalization will not suffice. To build the political and policy foundations for digital economies to expand and integrate, DVCs must first be constrained through coordinated *regulation* across countries.

Regulation is necessary because digital globalization raises a novel set of political conflicts and concerns emanating from DVC activities. First, the collection of personal information, a central input in digital services, raises privacy and other human rights concerns. Second, giant tech companies' market dominance leads to questions about competition and undue corporate political influence. Third, the increase in digitally enabled international services transactions strains an antiquated global tax system based on the production and sale of physical goods. Political conflicts arise because the global digital economy is missing institutional guardrails – the rules have not kept up with technology.

To alleviate sources of popular resistance to DVC activities, countries will need to coordinate around at least three main policy issues that the rules-based multilateral trade regime currently overlooks: privacy, competition, and taxation (see Figure 2). Absent global coordination in these areas, governments will continue to construct barriers to digital integration, further imperiling international economic cooperation.

This regulatory convergence requirement represents what I call the digital globalization paradox. For digital economies to integrate without political backlash, countries must build a common set of institutional foundations that constrain the activities of the most dominant digital firms. For digital globalization to achieve sustainable public support, it will require some convergence on policies for which cooperation has no precedent. Paradoxically, for digital globalization to flourish, the multinationals that currently dominate digital markets must first be restrained.

Creating the regulatory foundations for digital globalization will not be easy. International harmonization across such a wide domain of policies – privacy, competition, and taxation – has never been achieved, so there is no template for cooperation. Policymakers operate in a rules-based system built for trade in goods, which is ill-equipped to manage conflicts related to trade in digital products and services (Bacchus, 2022; Slaughter and McCormick, 2021). Developing a cooperative framework for the global digital economy will require building a consensus around a new set of rules that will constrain some of the activities of powerful firms. The outcome of conflicts over rules governing the digital economy will define international economic relations for the rest of this century.

The challenge for DVC firms is also immense. To succeed in the digital economy, firms must expand: economies of scale and scope drive growth. Gaining these size advantages often requires collecting and processing vast amounts of data. As I will show, political tension emanates from a business model that relies on a central input – data – for which global rules have yet to be written. Digital value chains have benefited from a permissive regulatory environment with undefined property rights over data. Weak institutions advantage first movers and incumbent DVC firms. When DVC firms get too big, their size and power inspire political demands for new regulations to constrain them. Politics will ultimately determine the rules for digital trade, and so digital firms will remain active political actors, monitoring and resisting policies that threaten their growth.

The task ahead for globalization scholars is complex. The data dimension in globalization challenges existing frameworks. I argue that digital globalization provokes new policy demands and reshuffles political coalitions in ways that workhorse models fail to explain. I introduce a new framework to explain the digital trade preferences of firms and individuals, and the digital governance strategies that countries pursue.

Crucially, the DVC generates political conflicts over policies that were previously considered distinct from international trade. Consumer data privacy is a new fault line that falls outside of standard political economy frameworks. Concerns about the erosion of human rights such as privacy arise alongside the technological capability to track, predict, and even influence individuals' behavior (Susskind, 2022; Véliz, 2020; Zuboff, 2019). These capabilities were virtually nonexistent when political economy models were developed to explain trade in goods. Existing political explanations for trade policy focus on narrow economic interests (Baccini et al., 2019; Frieden and Rogowski, 1996; Grossman and Helpman, 1994; Kim, 2017; Kim and Milner, 2019; Owen, 2017), but digital trade generates political demands and divisions that are sometimes motivated by noneconomic considerations, such as personal privacy.

At least three other political fault lines unique to the digital era emerge from the market consequences of DVCs. The first concerns the wealth and economic concentration generated by the economies of scale and network externalities unique to the data-driven economy (UNCTAD, 2019, 2021). The second fault line is multinationals' tax avoidance strategies. While not new to the digital economy, these strategies are made more effective by the ability to shift profits in digital intangibles like intellectual property, user data, and software (Aslam and Shah, 2021; Eden et al., 2019; UNCTAD, 2019). Finally, digital automation raises concerns over layoffs and the future of work, especially in the context of high industry concentration and wealth inequality. These novel political divisions force us to reassess the ways in which technology and business strategy shape international economic relations.

This Element does just that. It charts new directions for future research on the global politics of the digital economy and has four objectives: (1) to explain digital globalization and the new sources of political friction it creates; (2) to document the rise of policy barriers to international information flows; (3) to present a framework to explain digital trade restrictions across countries; and (4) to assess the prospects for international cooperation on digital governance.

This Element proceeds in four subsequent sections. Section 2 introduces the analytical framework from first principles: technology, the DVC, and the political controversies surrounding digital globalization. I demonstrate how new technologies facilitate the creation of data-driven business models centered on digital trade that can erode individual privacy, shift tax burdens, and cement monopoly positions. I argue that DVCs differ from goods value chains, and explain how these differences complicate the politics of globalization in the digital era.

Section 3 describes how governments have responded to the politics by developing policies to constrain digital globalization, including by restricting data flows, enacting privacy laws, and introducing digital services taxes (DSTs). I introduce a novel dataset that captures digital trade impediments around the world.

Section 4 develops a theoretical framework to explain how politics can account for variation in countries' divergent policy approaches. Charting a course for international cooperation and interoperability in the digital economy requires understanding how politics affects the digital trade policies that individual countries pursue. My theoretical approach does not privilege any single variable in explaining policy variation. Instead, it highlights a multitude of factors shaping digital trade restrictions, including the influence of powerful firms and coalitions, social norms and values, and political institutions.

Section 5 discusses the implications of countries' divergent approaches to digital governance. Unencumbered by rules, these policy differences threaten international economic cooperation. To overcome political resistance, digital globalization requires redesigning global regulatory institutions – a monumental task given the political divisions described here. This section lays out the institutional prerequisites for global cooperation in the digital era. It concludes with a discussion of topics for future research.

2 The Global Digital Economy

Digital globalization describes the integration of national digital economies. Data, software, and information and communication technologies (ICT) are changing the nature of goods and services that firms produce, and how firms interact with customers around the world. The international expansion of digital business models involves cross-border data and information flows, enabled by the Internet. This Element centers digital globalization in the cross-border economic activities of data-driven firms.

The driving force behind digital globalization is an economic structure called the DVC. A DVC transforms digital information into value. Digital information, or data, includes anything that can be encoded as bits (Goldfarb and Tucker, 2019; Shapiro et al., 1999). Through the collection, storage, and analysis of data, DVCs monetize information by converting it into services for sale either directly to consumers (business-to-consumers, B2C) or to other businesses (business-to-business (B2B)). These services include, among other things, a host of "digitally native" activities such as personalized advertising, market forecasting, e-commerce platform operations, and cloud services (UNCTAD, 2019). They also include traditional business services such as consulting, health care, and software services that are digitally delivered.

This section argues that the global expansion of DVCs creates novel political pressures – both within and across nations. My argument proceeds in three steps. First, I demonstrate how data, the central input into DVCs, differs from other economic inputs such as capital or labor. The distinguishing features of data help explain the second step of the argument: the digital economy is dominated by a small number of very large firms (the "digital giants"), which achieve and maintain their economic dominance by gathering personal information about individual consumers.

The novel forms of data-driven value creation ignite the politics of digital globalization. In the third step of the argument, I show that DVC activities reveal key institutional deficiencies related to the protection of personal privacy, the fairness of the global tax regime, economic inequality and concentration, and automation's impact on the future of work. These deficiencies threaten the integration of national digital economies – digital globalization – because they create incentives for governments to restrict data flows across borders in response to political pressures from their citizens. But before examining these policy restrictions and their political motivations, I introduce some conceptual foundations.

The Organization for Economic Co-operation and Development (OECD) defines *digital trade* as international transactions in goods and services that are digitally ordered or delivered (OECD, 2019). This definition includes e-commerce and the related platforms that enable retailers and service providers to reach consumers anywhere in the world. When combined with cloud computing, data generated in one country can be instantly stored and processed in another, to feed algorithms to more effectively target consumers. There is also a large B2B component of digital trade. For example, businesses digitally trade *intangibles* – including intellectual property, software, and data – with firms in other countries (Branstetter et al., 2019).[2] Trade in *data* is the fastest-growing aspect of globalization (Manyika et al., 2016).

Digital globalization includes trade in digitally enabled services, facilitated by the Internet. Digital platforms enable buyers and sellers to overcome an obstacle to services trade known as the *proximity burden*: unlike trade in goods, some services transactions require the consumer and the producer of the service to be in the same physical location (e.g., haircuts). Yet digital platforms, and technologies such as blockchain, a digital ledger of transactions, facilitate contractual relationships for services exchanged over the Internet. In this way, technology is alleviating the proximity burden of many services transactions (Baldwin, 2019; Jensen, 2011).

Figure 3 illustrates the share of digital services in total services exports among the world's largest economies.[3] It demonstrates that worldwide digitally deliverable services accounted for 63 percent of total services exports in

---

[2] According to one estimate, intangibles represent 84 percent of the value of the S&P 500, up from 17 percent in 1975 (source: https://tinyurl.com/tarqpbm).

[3] The data are from UNCTAD, and digitally deliverable services are "an aggregation of insurance and pension services, financial services, charges for the use of intellectual property, telecommunications, computer and information services, other business services and audiovisual and related services." These are UNCTAD calculations, based on UNCTAD and WTO datasets on international trade in services. See https://unctadstat.unctad.org/ for additional details.

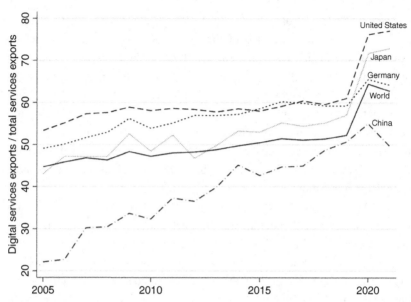

Figure 3 Digital services exports. Data from https://unctadstat.unctad.org/

2021, an increase of 40 percent since 2005. The figure also shows a massive 127 percent increase in China's digital services share since 2005. Also notable is the global uptick in 2020, which reflects how the COVID-19 pandemic accelerated the digital delivery of services (Borchert and Winters, 2021; Sarah, 2021).

Other international data transfers are not considered trade in the traditional sense. Valuable data often flows across borders and does not change ownership. New technologies allow cross-border data flows to expand. For instance, additive manufacturing relies on the digital transfer of information to create new products using 3D printers. In addition, Internet-of-Things (IoT) – consumer products that embed digital services capabilities into goods – are generating massive increases in data flows (Chander, 2019). The raw data generated by these products is potentially valuable, but their value is difficult to measure, and would not be included in trade statistics (Nguyen and Paczos, 2020). While the concept of digital trade does not include flows of raw data if they are unrelated to the specific exchange of a good or service (UNCTAD, 2021), such data flows are valuable to firms that can convert them into digital intelligence.

2.1 Data Fuels the Digital Economy

Data – information in digital form – is the central input in the digital economy. It fuels machine learning and other forms of artificial intelligence (AI) and automation that digitally oriented businesses use to optimize decisions and maximize profits. In this section, I discuss salient features of data and how it is used to create value. Like capital, labor, and land, data has become an important economic resource (Liu, 2021; UNCTAD, 2021). Yet it is unlike all other inputs in a couple of ways.

First, property rights over data have been difficult to establish and value. A central complication involves assigning ownership when both the data collector and the data subject can legitimately claim rightful ownership (Koutroumpis et al., 2020; World Bank, 2021). Another impediment is that the value of data can be difficult to assess before it is compiled in (typically) large volumes, processed, and analyzed in ways that provide new insights (Arrow, 1962).

The second way in which data is a unique input is that it is considered an intangible asset (a nonphysical resource that helps firms create value). Other examples of intangibles include licensing agreements, proprietary business processes and know-how, and other forms of intellectual property. Digitalization has led firms to place greater emphasis on monetizing intangibles; investment in intangibles now exceeds investment in physical capital in many advanced economies (Haskel and Westlake, 2018).

To illustrate its centrality and value to the information economy, data is often compared to oil. But data and oil differ in at least four relevant economic features (Scholz, 2018).

First, individual data are not inherently valuable. Individuals generally cannot create value with their personal data alone. To create value, data from many different economic or social transactions needs to be compiled and processed in ways that generate new insights that allow individuals, organizations, and businesses to make better decisions. For individuals to derive value from their data, at a minimum, individual property rights over data would need to be established and enforced.

Second, though its use can be excludable, data is generally considered to be nonrival in nature, in the sense that multiple entities can monetize the same dataset at the same time. This is because it is nearly costless to make a copy of an existing database. This feature of data – costless replicability – distinguishes it from commodities like oil and final goods like autos. Yet this does not prevent potential users from being legally or technically excluded: data can remain proprietary, usage can be restricted, and users can be excluded. Data are not a pure public good.

Third, data are nonfungible, meaning that one dataset is not interchangeable with another. Data used to automate specific tasks, or make predictions about certain outcomes, generally relies on related data that has measured similar outcomes in the past. If a business is interested in predicting future revenue, for example, a dataset of past revenue cannot be replaced with one containing unrelated information.

Finally, the most *politically* relevant feature of data is that it can be intimately linked to its subject, and transmitted at zero cost. Data on individuals can be collected, transferred, and analyzed to reveal deeply personal attributes, behaviors, and preferences in ways that can make it an ideal input into businesses' digital marketing strategies.

Data are increasingly valuable to firms and governments. For example, the deep insights into human behavior that AI can generate may motivate businesses and governments to exploit, surveil, and discriminate against certain individuals and groups. Along with private characteristics such as physical and mental health, data can be used to track where a person goes – and who they know. It can reveal individuals' economic and social standing, and record and predict their political behavior. Since data can capture increasingly specific and comprehensive details of individuals' thoughts, beliefs, actions, and preferences, personal data is the digital blueprint of one's *identity*.

Personal information can lead to discriminatory business practices. For example, firms rely on AI to decide which products and services align best with specific customers. The underlying data used to develop the predictive statistical models often does not adequately reflect the diversity of the population to which they are applied. In such cases, the training dataset is said to exhibit bias, which means that inferences are not reliable for underrepresented groups (DeBrusk, 2018). Left unaddressed, biased datasets can lead to discrimination in areas such as lending (Dobbie et al., 2018), hiring (Raghavan et al., 2020), and marketing (Lambrecht and Tucker, 2019).

I demonstrate that these distinguishing features of data give rise to a new form of globalization. Like earlier expansions of economic exchange, the global digital economy engenders political divisions and conflicts. However, the current digital politics involve a much broader set of issues than those linked to traditional trade in goods – including privacy regulation, taxation, and antitrust. Before we can understand these new issues of political contestation, however, we must first consider how DVCs, the economic engines driving digital globalization, convert data into value.

2.2 Digital Value Chains

Value chain analysis divides the process used to produce a good or service into discrete activities (Porter, 1985). The value chain concept was created to describe the sequential process that firms use to convert inputs into outputs in the production of manufactured goods (OECD, 2018). These sequential activities create new value by either generating differentiated products or reducing costs. Technology plays a central role in the global expansion of value chains. For instance, the Internet enabled firms to fragment their production processes across multiple countries to add value in what came to be called a global (manufacturing) value chain (GVC) (Baldwin, 2016; Gereffi and Fernandez-Stark, 2011; Hummels et al., 2001).

Global value chains mainly produce goods through a fragmented process that incorporates resources and creates value in multiple countries. Analogous to a global factory, GVC firms cooperate to produce and source parts, components, and service inputs in different countries to exploit differences in input costs (such as labor). Value is added in each link of the production chain.[4]

Technology is transforming trade in goods, services, and intangibles, and enabling a new form of value creation for businesses – the DVC. Digital value chains do not produce goods. They instead represent the process firms use to collect, store, analyze, and ultimately generate value by monetizing data – transforming digital information to produce new insights, known as digital intelligence (Nguyen and Paczos, 2020; UNCTAD, 2019). Digital value chains generate cross-border data flows whenever companies or consumers transfer data from servers in one country to those in another. Data is primarily an intermediate good in DVCs, which is often combined with other data and then transformed into valuable information, products, or services (Koutroumpis et al., 2020).[5]

Digital value chains generate value in multiple stages. Early stages involve collecting data. As an example, consider how some firms collect individual consumer data that comes from tracking clickstreams (or click paths). A clickstream is a digital record of a user's Internet activity, including site visits and purchases, time spent on a webpage, email and social media content, and contact information that a user sends or receives. Internet service providers collect clickstream data, and individual websites and platforms can record user information in text files called cookies. Data can be used to build a profile of individuals based on records of their digital activities.

In later stages, the DVC harnesses the value of data by storing, processing, and analyzing it (Li et al., 2019; Nguyen and Paczos, 2020). Machine-learning algorithms typically transform the data into digital intelligence, which may

---

[4] www.worldbank.org/en/topic/global-value-chains.

[5] Some studies have reconceptualized the value chain framework as a network to explain the fragmentation of digital services production (Stabell and Fjeldstad, 1998). For instance, Stabell and Fjeldstad (1998) explain how digital service providers rely on mediating technologies, such as online platforms, to link producers and consumers in what they refer to as their value networks approach.

include predictions about individual or market demand (Agrawal et al., 2018b; Brynjolfsson and McAfee, 2014; McAfee and Brynjolfsson, 2017).[6] This information about demand can be monetized through a variety of services, including targeted advertising. For instance, digitally native companies like Google and Meta/Facebook provide data-targeting services such as targeted online advertising and demand forecasting; they also license the information to third parties (Li et al., 2019). Digital adopters such as Walmart use data to optimize logistics and predict consumer demand. Firms strategically form DVCs to generate value when they monetize data to provide services, which in turn help them make better decisions, innovate, and reach new customers.

The following logic drives the success of DVCs: the more data, the better the predictions; the better the predictions, the more valuable the digital intelligence and the more data a business can obtain. Because popular platform companies collect so much information about individual users of their platforms and services, these companies can promise higher click conversions to advertisers, resulting in higher sales. Since data is nonrivalrous, or inexhaustible, value can be extracted repeatedly, even for different products or services (World Bank, 2021).

Figure 4 illustrates a stylized DVC. Data collection can occur in multiple countries, and the process of converting it into digital intelligence often involves cross-border data transfers. Digital services are then sold to consumers in other countries, which entails additional cross-border data flows.

Three main scientific advances have driven the rise of DVCs. The first is the exponential growth in computer processing speeds, without which algorithms would be unable to convert data into real-time digital intelligence (Baldwin, 2019; Brynjolfsson et al., 2019). The second innovation is the development of AI and machine learning – algorithms that convert data into intelligence. The third advance is the ability to collect and store large quantities of data, which machine-learning algorithms need in order to make the accurate predictions that are necessary to create value.

Platform businesses play a central role in the digital economy by facilitating commercial and social interactions between users. Following the OECD, I define an *online platform* as "a digital service that facilitates interactions between two or more distinct but interdependent sets of users (whether firms or individuals) who interact through the service via the Internet" (OECD, 2019). Platforms enable exchanges of goods, services, and information between users.

---

[6] Businesses generally either perform in-house data analytics or license data for use by other firms.

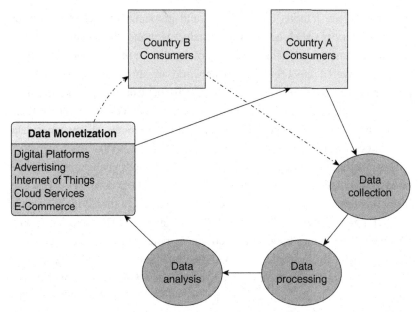

Figure 4 Digital value chains. Dashed lines represent cross-border data transfers. Adapted from UNCTAD (2021)

Online platforms can represent DVCs embedded in single firms. Platforms often conduct key stages of the data monetization process (data collection, storage, and analytics) in-house. The largest tech platforms invest in all stages of the DVC, including data collection; data transfer infrastructure such as submarine cables and satellites; data storage; and analysis and intelligence, such as AI (UNCTAD, 2021).

Online platforms can collect and analyze data about the interactions of all of their users – and monetize this data by selling it to third parties, or using it as an input for value-generating algorithms. Data monetization gives platforms a key source of growth. For instance, Amazon analyzes clickstreams, customer locations, purchases, and review data to generate demand forecasts, which they sell to third parties as logistics consulting services (Li et al., 2019).[7] Apple charges app developers 30 percent commissions for access to its consumer data, which has generated over $40 billion in revenue in less than a decade (Frier, 2018).

While the digital economy is often associated with leading platform firms, businesses across all sectors increasingly rely on digital business models.

---

[7] Amazon can charge $100,000 per year for this service alone. www.ft.com/content/c82ce968-bc8a-11e8-94b2-17176fbf93f5.

For instance, the Internet enables firms and individuals to remotely deliver a range of services such as software development and management consulting – which has expanded the offshoring of the service sector (Baldwin, 2019). Services delivered remotely over ICT networks are known as digitally deliverable (or ICT-enabled) services (UNCTAD, 2019).[8] Consumer goods are now also firmly integrated into DVCs. For instance, IoT devices such as smart thermostats allow firms to collect and analyze untold amounts of consumer data that can be monetized as digital intelligence (Chander, 2019).

This integration of digital services and physical goods challenges the rules-based global trading system. Within the World Trade Organization (WTO), the distinction between goods and services is fundamental to specifying the extent to which trade is liberalized or restricted (Azmeh et al., 2020; Sen, 2018). For example, a hardbound book is a good and is potentially subject to customs duties, whereas an electronic version of the same book is considered a service, subject to General Agreement on Trade in Services (GATS) rules, which currently include a moratorium on e-commerce customs duties (Sen, 2018). Yet the WTO does not clearly distinguish goods from services, and many innovative electronic products exhibit features of both. Trade in goods is subject to clear rules and tariff schedules. But the IoT, which confer substantial added value to the product, are data-dependent services, and are not subject to the same trade rules (Azmeh et al., 2020; Sen, 2018).

Section 2.3 explores the second salient political feature of digital markets: a small set of extraordinarily large firms dominates them. I explain how data has facilitated the rise of these digital giants, and why the concentration of digital markets is politically sensitive.

2.3 The Global Digital Giants

Digital markets exhibit high degrees of concentration: a small number of firms account for a disproportionately high share of production and sales. Market concentration tends to be a global, rather than domestic, phenomenon. Digital technologies blur geographic boundaries, which enables a small number of firms to dominate global markets. The Internet facilitates instantaneous digital economic exchange with global scope, particularly for digital services. In traditional markets, frictions related to distance (like transportation costs) still impede trade (Disdier and Head, 2008; Hummels and Schaur, 2013). In

---

[8] Digital-deliverable services are categorized by UNCTAD as "insurance and pension services, financial services, charges for the use of intellectual property, telecommunications, computer and information services, other business services and audiovisual and related services" (see https://unctadstat.unctad.org/wds/TableViewer/summary.aspx?ReportId=158358).

goods markets, transportation costs constrain the economies of scale linked to physical production, meaning that concentration is often localized at the regional or national scale. Digital markets lack these traditional geographic constraints, since data can – at least in principle and absent policy restrictions – flow costlessly around the planet.

Market concentration within countries is high, but the *geographic* concentration of digital power in the United States and China is truly extraordinary. The vast majority of the largest tech firms are domiciled in either the United States or China. Around 90 percent of Internet searches are made through Google; Amazon makes up nearly 40 percent of online retail; and Amazon Web Services accounts for nearly 30 percent of the rapidly growing cloud computing market.[9] Facebook became the most popular media platform in over 90 percent of countries. Alibaba accounts for 60 percent of China's e-commerce, and Alipay (owned by Alibaba) dominates the mobile payments market (UNCTAD, 2019).

In this section I explain the causes of digital market concentration: network effects, Big Tech's aggressive acquisition strategies, and economies of scale and scope. Although some of these features are present in traditional (nondigital) markets, their combination and ubiquity across the digital economy is unique (Furman et al., 2019). I then briefly highlight some of the market consequences of concentration, and then detail how digital markets spur political conflict.

Several features of digital markets help explain their concentration, but consumer data are central to most explanations (Furman et al., 2019; Lancieri and Sakowski, 2021). Firms obtain data through the market interactions of their users, and network effects (i.e., the more users who join a platform, the more valuable it becomes) help create first-mover advantages and winner-takes-all competition (Borchert and Winters, 2021). More users and more data allow first movers to outperform potential upstarts – further cementing their market dominance (UNCTAD, 2019) and "tipping" markets in favor of the dominant provider.

Leading firms obtain more data because they attract more users, and the data tends to be of higher quality – that is, it covers market interactions with greater granularity and frequency. And better data allows the algorithms powering digital firms to create more accurate inferences about consumer preferences and behavior. Higher-quality data also helps firms provide new and better services (such as better search functions, more accurate directed marketing, and

---

[9] www.parkmycloud.com/blog/aws-vs-azure-vs-google-cloud-market-share/.

other personalized services), which strengthens the competitive positions of dominant firms.

Digital giants' acquisition strategies, driven by competitive threats and the need to collect vast amounts of data, also generate high levels of market concentration. In what are known as pre-emptive mergers, major tech players purchase potential competitors offering similar or complementary services before the companies can become a competitive threat – and before the acquisition risks rejection by regulators for reducing competition (Stiglitz, 2019).

Sometimes the promise of acquiring troves of proprietary customer data motivates digital giants to purchase smaller companies. Microsoft purchased professional social network LinkedIn for $26 billion – more than $60 per registered user – in part to access data on its hundreds of millions of members. Combined with the information it has about individual customers, Microsoft could use the LinkedIn data to fuel machine-learning tools to boost advertising and marketing sales.[10] In another example, Amazon famously absorbed losses of $200 million per month to undercut the prices on Diapers.com to weaken the rival (Lancieri and Sakowski, 2021) so Amazon could acquire it.[11] This practice is sometimes deemed predatory pricing – lowering prices to drive out or potentially absorb rivals. The consolidation of data resources among the major digital platforms and technology firms helps establish their market dominance and increases their concentration (UNCTAD, 2019).

Data also helps generate economies of scale and scope in digital markets, which further contributes to concentrated markets dominated by a handful of firms (Furman et al., 2019; Lancieri and Sakowski, 2021; Moore and Tambini, 2018). For businesses, costs depend on how much firms produce. The cost structure of digital markets entails high initial (fixed) costs for software development and investments in digital infrastructure. However, once the infrastructure and software are in place, the marginal costs of reaching new customers are next to nothing. Network effects further increase these large returns to scale. Firms with expertise in data analytics can use their software and data resources to develop new products and services at lower costs. If the combination of multiple datasets yields insights that are unavailable using a single type of data, economies of scope can expand further (World Bank, 2021). Their data resources allow firms to enjoy economies of scope by creating a range of new products using existing resources.

Data-driven economies of scale and scope can catapult business growth and competitiveness into a positive feedback loop, in which more (and better) data

---

[10] www.marketingweek.com/microsofts-linkedin-acquisition-is-a-data-and-advertising-play/.

[11] www.bloomberg.com/news/articles/2020-07-29/amazon-emails-show-effort-to-weaken-diapers-com-before-buying-it.

leads to new products and services that facilitate the collection of still more data (Iansiti and Lakhani, 2020). AI applications enable firms to translate that data into increasingly accurate inferences about the tastes of their own consumers – and into predictions of market demand, including among consumers not in their databases. When data is a key asset that is inaccessible to competitors, it can bestow a nearly unassailable advantage on incumbents, creating a barrier to entry for potential new rivals and reducing competition (Furman et al., 2019; Iansiti and Lakhani, 2020).

Without a data property rights regime that lets individuals own their own data, the companies capable of collecting and analyzing data are the ones that control (and extract value from) it (Aslam and Shah, 2021). The digital companies and platforms with the most users therefore enjoy enormous economic advantages.

The concentration of digital markets risks undermining competition, defined as the process rival firms use to obtain and maintain customers. Consumers benefit from competition among multiple businesses offering similar products, since rivalry creates incentives to respond to consumer preferences, create new products, and maintain high quality and low prices. Market competition tends to increase productivity as well, since it induces firms to optimize the use of their resources by learning how to create more outputs with fewer inputs (Furman et al., 2019). However, when a market contains high levels of concentration and few rivals, firms may raise prices above levels that would prevail in competitive markets, without causing consumers to purchase from rival firms.

Digital markets may enable businesses to deploy *market power* to their strategic advantage. A business has market power if it can independently influence the market price of its products. For instance, market power enables platforms to boost their own-brand sales without losing market share to rivals selling on their platform; platforms' access to data on third-party transactions allows them to optimize this approach.

Market power is politically controversial, especially if firms from other countries are allowed to dominate domestic markets through means that are deemed unfair or predatory. For example, the EU competition authorities are cracking down on what they view as unfair practices stemming from Amazon's market power. Its platform enables market transactions between buyers and sellers. For some products, Amazon is also a seller. The platform uses digital intelligence derived from sales on its platform to price its own products for strategic advantage, sometimes undercutting its competitors. This practice violates European competition policy, and the EU authorities have initiated legal action against Amazon in response.

This example illustrates how structural features of the digital economy give rise to novel policy considerations. Industrial concentration and alleged anti-competitive practices link digital globalization directly to competition policy – the rules governing market competition and responses to monopolistic behavior, which vary significantly by country (Weymouth, 2016). Competition authorities are not subject to harmonized rules, since there is no multilateral competition policy agreement. As I demonstrate in the next section, the contentious politics of digital globalization follow disparate approaches to its governance.

2.4 Politically Contentious Features of the Digital Economy

Consumers benefit from the digital economy in many ways, including greater product variety, more efficient matching to producers, and vast amounts of information available at just a click away. Many of these benefits are available at zero monetary cost; consumers instead exchange their personal data for free services such as search engines, e-commerce, social media, and maps. These services are estimated to be worth several thousand dollars a year to the typical user (Brynjolfsson et al., 2019). The global reach and popularity of online platforms suggests large consumer welfare surpluses from the digital economy (Furman et al., 2019). These benefits, however, mask deep political divides.

The digital economy ignites political backlash around a host of issues, particularly personal privacy, tax fairness, inequality, and automation. I argue in this section that politically contentious aspects of the era of digital globalization stem from key features of the DVC. Without coordinated regulation to constrain the more politically contentious outcomes identified here, digital globalization will create political strife within and among countries.

2.4.1 Erosion of Individual Privacy and Agency

Privacy is the state of being free from observation by others. It is unrelated to economic constructs such as employment or income, which anchor many explanations of individual trade policy preferences. Individual privacy concerns therefore fall outside traditional political economy frameworks, which tend to focus on economic distributional issues.

Growth in the digital economy is at odds with personal privacy. As businesses increasingly rely on digital technologies to collect granular user data, individual insularity and freedom from participation in the digital economy disintegrates. The DVC relies on surveillance of all forms of behavior, recorded through clicks, sensors, and GPS. Businesses are constantly seeking more granular information about consumers.

Companies can profit from users' personal information because property rights do not exist for most types of personal data. Since individual users do not own their own data, companies can collect, store, analyze, and monetize personal information to create targeted marketing strategies and new services. The more the data reveals about consumers, the more valuable it is. Privacy-related considerations also include data breaches and coercive tactics fueled by data-driven algorithms.

Digital markets expose consumers and businesses to the risk of various forms of data loss. Data breach refers to the intentional or inadvertent exposure of confidential information to unauthorized parties (Cheng et al., 2017). Breaches can endanger personal information, such as social security and driver's license numbers, as well as employment, health, and financial information. Businesses also risk losing intellectual property to online hackers. Cybercrime is estimated to cost businesses trillions of dollars each year, driven in part by increases in regulatory fines and lawsuits in response to data losses.[12]

Many traditional goods and services now have the capacity for digital connectivity and data extraction. For instance, billions of physical IoT devices are embedded with data-gathering sensors and software and linked to wireless networks. These connected devices – from refrigerators to home security systems – constantly collect, store, and share detailed personal information. For the systems to function optimally, consumers are usually unable to opt out. For businesses to fully maximize the value of the technology, IoT requires the ability to transfer data across borders, combine it with other data sources, and analyze the combined data, often in the headquarters country (Chander, 2019; Meltzer, 2019).

Many digital products are principally designed and implemented to allow companies to access personal data from as many sources as possible. Shoshana Zuboff describes the constant monitoring of individual behavior in the digital economy as a system of "surveillance capitalism" centered on the commodification and monetization of personal data (Zuboff, 2019). Along with the loss of individual privacy, surveillance capitalism can threaten liberty and well-being.

AI applications' ability to nudge consumer behavior implies an evolution of marketing and sales tactics that may move beyond persuasion and toward a form of *coercion*. One metric of successful commercial machine learning is the ability to correctly predict individual preferences and consumer demand. However, the most profitable digital firms use personal data not just to predict consumer behavior, but also to *influence* it. Businesses have always used marketing tactics to persuade customers to purchase their products, but these were

---

[12] www.juniperresearch.com/press/press-releases/business-losses-cybercrime-data-breaches.

never as personalized, or nearly as effective, as those made possible through machine learning. And personalized advertising is just the beginning.

The current frontier of commercial AI effectively "unlocks" consumer demand: it works to *affect* consumer behavior (Mele et al., 2021). Zuboff (2019) quotes the chief data scientist of a large US corporation as saying: "You can make people do things with this technology. Even if it's just five percent of people, you've made five percent of people do an action they otherwise wouldn't have done, so to some extent there is an element of the user's loss of self-control" (Zuboff, 2019, p. 19). Another data scientist boasted, "we can engineer the context around a particular behavior and force change that way. We are learning how to write the music, and then we let the music make them dance" (Zuboff, 2019, p. 295). While the disintegration of privacy in the digital economy threatens consumer welfare, it may only represent the means to a more troubling erosion of individual agency.

Individuals are increasingly concerned about privacy and how technology erodes it. In a recent global CIGI-Ipsos survey, 78 percent of respondents expressed concern about their online privacy.[13] In another survey conducted by Pew in the United States, 81 percent of respondents indicated that the potential risks of companies collecting data about them outweighed the benefits.[14] Roughly three-quarters (76 percent) think there should be more government regulation of what companies can do with their customers' personal data. And unlike most issues in the United States, there is strikingly little partisan division over personal data regulation: 81 percent of Democrats and 70 percent of Republicans would like increased government regulation of personal data privacy.

Privacy is a particularly thorny obstacle to building a cooperative framework for the global digital economy. The value that individuals place on their privacy differs across countries, and is continuously evolving (Farrell and Newman, 2019b). For instance, the notion that privacy represents a human right is not universally accepted even across democracies, to say nothing of rampant surveillance and privacy abuses under many authoritarian regimes (Dragu and Lupu, 2021). A further complication is that the politics of privacy evolve in response to changes in technology and the associated norms (Farrell and Newman, 2019b; Newman, 2008a,b). Technologies that feed personal information into algorithms designed to manipulate consumer behavior are becoming increasingly controversial as consumers recognize the invasiveness and scope

---

[13] www.cigionline.org/internet-survey-2019.

[14] www.pewresearch.org/internet/2019/11/15/americans-and-privacy-concerned-confused-and-feeling-lack-of-control-over-their-personal-information/.

of digital surveillance (Kröger et al., 2021; MacKinnon, 2012; Véliz, 2020; Zuboff, 2019).

Individual privacy concerns – not citizen preferences derived from group identities or the economic distributional effects of trade – may be the essential impediment to global cooperation on digital globalization. Building consumers' trust in the security of personal information will be a central challenge to commercial cooperation in the digital era (Cowhey and Aronson, 2017). To garner the necessary political support for digital globalization, major economies will likely need to coordinate on a baseline level of consumer privacy protections.

2.4.2 The Obsolescing Global Taxation Regime

The digital economy exerts new pressures on antiquated international tax rules. The current global tax framework originated in the 1920s, when firms and production were largely immobile. The framework consists of domestic tax law, tax treaties, and other instruments of international law, built upon assumptions regarding the residence of the corporation and the source of its income that do not apply today (OECD, 2018). One assumption is that of sharp boundaries around business activity: activity occurs within clear jurisdictional boundaries; firms reach customers by locating within these specified boundaries; and income is allocated between countries where sales occur. A second assumption is that businesses sell to customers from physical locations.

From these assumptions emerges the nexus rule: the country in which income-producing *physical* activity occurs has the primary right to tax. A country's tax base from corporate income refers to its right to tax the net profits of physical corporations. The market country where sales occur, in contrast, has no taxing rights except for sales taxes charged to consumers (Djankov, 2021).

One implication is that most governments collect zero taxes on the billions of dollars in digital services revenue generated in their jurisdictions by the digital giants. Digitalization allows firms to achieve international "scale without mass" (OECD, 2018): physical and territorial boundaries need not limit the exchange of goods and services. Thus, DVC business models can generate income in countries without contributing to their tax bases at all (Eden et al., 2019). The digital economy fundamentally challenges the international framework on corporate income taxation.

Digital technologies also facilitate tax evasion and related profiteering through at least two types of creative electronic transactions that exploit gaps and mismatches in global tax rules: transfer pricing and intangibles sales (Djankov, 2021). Transfer pricing is when a company makes costs appear bigger in high-tax countries and revenues appear bigger in low-tax countries. An estimated 40 percent of multinationals' global profits are artificially shifted to low-tax countries (Tørsløv et al., 2018). The tax minimizing logic of intangibles sales is similar: firms sell expensive intangibles like patents and software from a subsidiary in a low-tax country to another in a high-tax country, increasing costs in the high-tax jurisdiction and increasing profits in the low-tax jurisdiction (Aslam and Shah, 2021; Djankov, 2021; Zucman, 2015).

By increasing the volume, salience, and value of intangibles, digital globalization enables tax avoidance. Tax authorities are well aware of the sort of tax manipulations that firms pursue, but prosecution is rare because illegality is difficult to prove. For one thing, intangible assets are very difficult to value from a distance. Firms recognize the value of their intangible assets, but outside authorities may not. Digital value chain reliance on intangible assets such as data, software, patents, and other IP complicates taxation and its enforcement since the value and location of these assets can be opaque.

As public awareness of multinational tax avoidance grows, demands that firms contribute their fair share are increasing (Sandbu, 2019), and governments are resorting to new types of tax policies that target DVCs. For instance, numerous EU officials invoke transfer pricing and the absence of local hiring by US tech companies to justify their digital tax proposals, which would mainly affect large US firms. Indeed, a patchwork of new DSTs is emerging around the world as countries pursue ad hoc approaches to broaden their tax revenues. The next section examines these new DSTs and introduces a new dataset capturing developments in DSTs around the world.

The threat of DSTs has led to calls to reform the global tax system. In June 2021, the OECD developed a new framework for the taxation of MNCs, which 136 nations signed onto. The deal bans DSTs for two years, after which a 15 percent minimum corporate tax rate would come into effect, as well as new rules that would force MNCs to declare profits and pay more taxes in countries where they do business. National governments must pass the measure for it to be implemented, and in the United States, opposition by the US Chamber of Commerce may derail its passage.[15] If Congress fails to implement the deal, countries may impose or reinstate DSTs.

2.4.3 Economic Concentration, Inequality, and Digital Imperialism

A third area of contention involves the economic dominance and political influence of the global digital giants. Certain features of the DVC, including the

---

[15] www.bloomberg.com/news/articles/2022-02-15/u-s-chamber-s-bradley-raises-concern-over-global-tax-deal.

propensity for network effects and the rapid accrual of economies of scale and scope, enable a small number of firms to dominate their markets, meaning that fewer firms account for a larger share of profits.

Yet market concentration impedes entry by potential competitors, which stifles competition and further entrenches market and political power at the expense of consumer welfare. Economic power can translate into political influence if entrenched incumbent firms can capture regulators through campaign contributions, lobbying, or other tactics (Weymouth, 2012). Digital value chains may therefore not only concentrate *economic* might; they may also establish and foment domestic and international political power in the hands of a small number of corporations.

The rising concentration of digital industries coincides with a marked increase in economic inequality. Corporate concentration and inequality could be linked through at least four channels (Furman and Orszag, 2018). First, market power allows firms to charge higher prices than they could if there were more firms competing in the market. The resulting decline in *consumer surplus* – the difference between what they would be willing to pay for a product and what they pay in a competitive market – represents a transfer of wealth from consumers to businesses and their shareholders. Moreover, digital businesses' ability to accurately predict how much any consumer is willing to pay allows them to price discriminate – to charge different prices to different consumers.

In a second possible channel, just as market power allows firms to raise prices, concentration and market power in labor markets enables them to pay lower wages than they would otherwise (Stiglitz, 2019). This fact, along with the decline in union participation in recent decades, has led to lower labor shares of national income (Dorn et al., 2017).

A third channel through which the digital economy could increase inequality is automation and job displacement, which I discuss in more detail below. If automation is labor displacing, this reduces the demand for labor, and wages must fall to restore full employment. If automation is more likely to displace lower-skilled workers then wages will fall, or grow more slowly, for workers at the lower end of the income distribution, causing inequality to rise (Korinek and Stiglitz, 2019; Stiglitz, 2019).

The fourth, and perhaps most pernicious, consequence of market power operates through the political system. Market power bestows outsized political influence on the largest firms (Khan, 2018; Teachout and Khan, 2014), leading to lower corporate tax rates and other regulatory liberalizations that benefit them at the expense of the broader public, sometimes perpetuating inequality. Technological advances, such as those driving digital globalization, may tilt the balance of power away from the state toward the largest firms (Strange, 1997).

How does economic power translate into political influence? The obvious mechanism is that successful firms have more resources to spend on lobbying policymakers. Firms may lobby to shape or forestall new regulations, such as digital privacy laws, or to maintain favorable tax policies. Multinationals are more likely than domestic firms to lobby (Kim and Osgood, 2019), and political contributions have been found to result in lower effective tax rates for those that engage in lobbying (Richter et al., 2009). However, businesses usually spend only a small fraction of their sales on lobbying – so little that some scholars find the *lack* of money in politics puzzling (Ansolabehere et al., 2003). For instance, although Alphabet's lobbying expenditure in the United States was just 0.005 percent of its total revenue in 2020,[16] it actively participates in politics and exerts substantial political influence (Bank et al., 2021). But lobbying spending and campaign contributions are not the only way that corporate titans can achieve their policy objectives.

Powerful companies can also pursue at least three types of alternative strategies to influence policy (Zingales, 2017). First, they can operate through the legal system, filing lawsuits against unfavorable regulatory actions. Second, they can avoid regulation by directly lobbying the regulators who enforce the requirements. Third, firms can hide crucial information to avoid costly enforcement and oversight. Political power is on display when businesses secure favorable treatment or avoid costly regulation, regardless of how much they spend on formally registered lobbying activities.

Size and market concentration enhance the effectiveness of all sorts of firms' policy influence strategies. In general, political influence increases with market concentration (Olson, 1965), which makes large corporations more powerful relative to consumers (Weymouth, 2016; Zingales, 2017). To the extent that consumer interests differ from the regulatory ambitions of the digital giants, concentration is generally assumed to give businesses a political advantage. As the size and market shares of businesses increase, there are fewer firms in the industry with conflicting interests (Jensen et al., 2015), which helps unify the lobbying effort (Baccini et al., 2019; Macher and Mayo, 2015; Weymouth, 2012).

Yet the digital economy can reshuffle political alliances. Consumer interests do not always conflict with those of dominant firms. The prevalence of free products and network externalities common to DVCs complicates standard frameworks of regulatory politics (Culpepper and Thelen, 2020). The prevailing approach pits consumer interests against producers with pricing power

---

[16] Open Secrets reports Alphabet's lobbying expenditure was \$8,850,000 and its total revenue was \$182 billion.

(Peltzman, 1976; Rogowski and Kayser, 2002). But in the digital economy, the free services that digital platforms provide may lead consumers to side with the tech giants in opposition to some forms of regulation. This "tacit allegiance" of consumers provides a formidable source of opposition to regulations that threaten the digital giants (Culpepper and Thelen, 2020).

For example, a dispute between Facebook and the Australian government arose over a proposed law requiring platforms to pay news organizations for posted stories. Facebook expressed its opposition to the law by blocking user access to Australian news, including some Australian government communications content.[17] The company bet that its millions of loyal users in the country would side with it. The pressure worked, and the Australian government agreed to amend the law. Facebook's political power was heightened by the alliance with its users. The spat signaled that the company could successfully deploy hardball tactics with user support if faced with similar regulatory stances by governments in other countries.

Digital giants' ability to coerce governments and extract data resources has led some analysts and activists to decry the dangers of undue corporate influence. Some have warned that digital globalization is ushering in a new era of colonialism and imperialism, in which US and Chinese firms collect, extract, and monetize data from other countries, which cements their monopoly positions and restricts entry and competition from smaller upstarts (Avila Pinto, 2018; Kwet, 2019; Wasik, 2015). The central concern is that developing countries will become mere subordinate providers of raw data for the global digital giants, which control (and thus capture the vast majority of the value from) this data (UNCTAD, 2021).

This fear has led to new calls for countries to exert their *digital sovereignty* by restricting data extraction and creating shared infrastructures to allow domestic firms to share data resources. Digital sovereignty describes "a state's sovereign power to regulate not only cross-border flow of data through uses of Internet filtering technologies and data localization mandates, but also speech activities (e.g., combating fake news) and access to technologies" (Chander and Sun, 2021, p.10). In many countries, it seeks to thwart the digital dominance of US businesses, which have amassed substantial market shares across a range of digital activities over the past couple of decades. Former German Chancellor Angela Merkel and other leaders from Europe to India have called for digital sovereignty, seeking to wrest control of domestic user data back from Silicon Valley, and to develop cloud technologies to collect and store it (Chazan, 2019).

---

[17] https://apnews.com/article/google-facebook-australia-explained-55ce7a524855c2cdabdf8ca8 2ad2c8cd.

2.4.4 Digital Automation, Layoffs, and the Future of Work

Data-centered business models involve cost-cutting automation – replacing humans with machines to perform routine tasks (Brynjolfsson and McAfee, 2014). The trend toward digital automation risks a future of weaker labor demand as more companies rely on AI and robotics. Frey and Osborne (2017) estimate that computerized automation will put nearly half (47 percent) of US jobs at risk of elimination over the next two decades. Whether digital automation will lead to the elimination of millions of jobs remains unknown, but many analysts are deeply concerned (Baldwin, 2019; Frey, 2019; Frey and Osborne, 2017).

Others argue that AI and other forms of automation generate beneficial productivity effects that can offset the impact of job losses (Acemoglu and Restrepo, 2019; Agrawal et al., 2019; David, 2015). Offsetting benefits of automation operate through two channels (Acemoglu and Restrepo, 2019). First, automation reduces costs and leads to lower prices for goods and services that are automated, increasing real household incomes, and expanding demand across the economy. Second, the introduction of new labor-intensive tasks that AI is (currently) unable to do will create new jobs. Thus, the magnitude of job losses will depend on the extent to which the displacing effects of automation are offset by higher productivity and the increased demand for workers in new, labor-intensive tasks.

Digital globalization also introduces *international* competition for jobs that technology has yet to automate. As Baldwin (2019) explains, online platforms linking employers and workers, coupled with instant translation and video conferencing, make previously nontradable services fully contestable by workers in other countries. Baldwin (2019) contends that the offshoring of white-collar jobs will ignite a backlash among professional services workers in high-wage countries.

Governments have strong incentives to closely monitor and implement policies to address the labor market effects of digital automation and services offshoring, since labor market shocks expose worker vulnerabilities in ways that influence political behavior (Gallego and Kurer, 2022). Previous research has illustrated that economic shocks caused by globalization initiated a voter backlash against incumbents and mainstream candidates (Ahlquist et al., 2020; Baccini and Weymouth, 2021; Ballard-Rosa et al., 2021; Colantone and Stanig, 2018a; Dorn et al., 2020; Jensen et al., 2017; Rickard, 2021), which pushed the United States and other nations to rethink their commitment to a liberal international order (Broz et al., 2021; Colantone and Stanig, 2018b; Mansfield and Rudra, 2021; Milner, 2021; Owen and Walter, 2017; Walter, 2021). The possibility of an automation-induced labor market upheaval could similarly upend politics.

There is evidence that anxieties around the future of work are already altering political behavior and elections. Exposure to automation increases worker anxiety in ways similar to trade and outsourcing, and recent evidence finds strong political reactions among affected voters through three channels. First, technological changes may weaken trust in the merits of democracy (Boix, 2019; Gilardi, 2022) and globalization (Iversen and Soskice, 2019; Mansfield et al., 2021; Wu, 2021). Second, middle-class employment anxieties associated with automation may inspire political conflict and support for populist candidates (Frey et al., 2018; Frey, 2019; Gidron and Hall, 2017; Gingrich, 2019; Im et al., 2019; Kurer, 2020). For instance, voters may find right-wing populist messages appealing if susceptibility to automation makes them anxious about their social status and position in the social hierarchy (Baccini and Weymouth, 2021; Gidron and Hall, 2017; Jardina, 2019; Kurer, 2020). Third, workers at risk of losing their jobs to automation could favor policies to slow down technological change, including the regulation and taxation of worker-displacing innovations such as robotics (Gallego et al., 2021; Thewissen and Rueda, 2019). Workers who are vulnerable to the vicissitudes of the digital economy may also favor digital trade barriers like those discussed in the next section.

In summary, this new era of digital globalization is driven by the DVC, in which data is the central input. Yet property rights over data are not well established. Technology converts data into computational intelligence, prediction, and automation, which gives firms enormous power to forecast market demand, cut production costs, and monitor and coerce consumers. Digital value chains contribute to extremely high industrial and geographic concentration, with industries dominated by a handful of very large firms. These firms dominate global markets, yet their sales often go untaxed. There is not yet a global, rules-based system governing the digital economy, and political tensions are on the rise due in no small part to digital firms' exorbitant economic and political power.

These controversial aspects of DVCs place digital globalization at a crossroads; politics will determine its outcome. Surveillance capitalism, economic concentration, and tax avoidance are inducing a popular backlash. In response to political pressures from their citizens, governments around the world are enacting new laws and regulations that impede data flows across borders. These digital trade impediments reflect a host of political pressures and concerns unique to the digital era. For governments wishing to exert control over data and information flows – in other words, to establish *digital sovereignty* – one lever is to impede data extraction and value creation by restricting cross-border data flows.

The next section surveys the digital trade impediments governments are devising in an attempt to constrain the most politically contentious features of digital globalization. I then turn to the domestic and international politics of digital globalization. Section 4 develops a framework to explain variation in policy impediments to digital flows. Section 5 defines the paradox of digital globalization and the prospects for international cooperation on the governance of the digital economy.

3 Policy Impediments to Digital Globalization

Governments around the world are governing DVCs with a new policy activism, which I document in this section. Since the WTO and other multilateral institutions generally do not proscribe policy obstacles to digital trade, countries are relatively unconstrained in their policy choices. The absence of an agreement on standards and rules for cross-border data flows permits significant digital trade policy discretion.

Governments have implemented various policies that restrict certain aspects of digital trade and data transfers in order to ensure a desired degree of protection or surveillance. There is no single policy mechanism, akin to a tariff in goods trade, to achieve governments' varying objectives. Instead, governments often pursue a patchwork of barriers to cross-border data flows that increase the costs of firms' global activities (Casalini et al., 2021; Hodson, 2019). Casalini et al. (2021) calculate that 82 percent of policies affecting digitally enabled services around the world between 2014 and 2019 were trade *restricting*, while only 18 percent were trade *liberalizing*. These new digital trade barriers – which include data privacy laws, cybersecurity laws, digital taxes, and various regulatory impediments to digital services and e-commerce – have increased markedly in recent years (Aaronson, 2021; Casalini and González, 2019; Ferracane and Lee-Makiyama, 2018).[18]

Some refer to these restrictions on data flows as "digital protectionism," although there is no consensus on a definition among scholars or policymakers (Aaronson and Leblond, 2018). In the context of international trade, protectionism broadly refers to policy measures that restrict the supply or increase the cost of imports.

I avoid the term "protectionism" when discussing digital trade policies because it implies a desire to shield, or protect, domestic firms from foreign

---

[18] An even more expansive view of barriers includes policies to limit disinformation, censorship, cybersecurity laws, and Internet shutdowns (Aaronson, 2021).

competition. Yet some restrictions on data flows may seek to protect individual privacy, for instance, rather than advantage domestic companies; this is not a protectionist motive. Moreover, unlike the general acceptance of the benefits of tariff liberalization, there is currently no consensus on best practices for digital trade policy, which are likely to depend on specific industry structures and other economic and political contexts (Borchert and Winters, 2021). I use the term *digital trade restrictions* to describe the set of policies that impede, or raise the costs of, digital trade.

This section evaluates the three main types of digital trade restrictions employed by governments around the world: (1) data flow restrictions, (2) data localization requirements, and (3) DSTs. It analyzes a novel digital trade restrictions database I created for this study, which records digital flow restrictions and digital taxes.[19] I also draw on three additional databases. The first is Ferracane and Lee-Makiyama (2018)'s Digital Trade Restrictiveness Index, which represents one of the first attempts to measure regulatory policies related to data. The second is the OECD's Digital Services Trade Restrictiveness Index, which quantifies cross-cutting barriers that affect digital services trade in forty-four countries (Ferencz, 2019). Third, Chander and Schwartz (2022) document national privacy laws with GDPR-adjacent adequacy-type standards for data exports.

3.1 Data Flow Restrictions

Data flow restrictions are policies that impede the movement of data across borders. Some restrictions apply to all types of information, whereas others are targeted to certain types of data or particular sectors of the economy. Among the most common restrictions are those applied to personal data, or information about an identifiable person. Governments also restrict the international transfer of other types of information such as business records, financial data, and government data. Since DVCs primarily monetize personal data, I focus on data flow restrictions pertaining to this type of information.

Data flow restrictions, like other trade impediments, raise the costs of global business. Costs increase when companies are forced to store data in a particular country, or when firms must comply with additional hurdles before transferring data abroad (Ferracane, 2017; Mattoo and Meltzer, 2018). There is substantial variation in the overall restrictiveness of data flow regulations around the

---

[19] The sources for data flow restrictions include USTR, Comforte, the ECIPE DTRI (Ferracane and Lee-Makiyama, 2018), DLA Piper, Chen (2021), and Cory and Dascoli (2021). Data on DSTs comes from KPMG and Alavara.

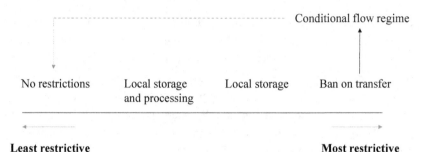

Figure 5 Types of cross-border data transfer restrictions. Adapted from Ferracane (2017)

world. As of 2022, my database records 133 data flow restriction laws either passed or proposed in 104 countries. Some require local storage and strictly prohibit the transfer of personal information outside of the home country. Two types of regulations are increasingly common: cross-border flow restrictions (usually as part of data privacy regulation), and local storage requirements (Casalini and González, 2019). Some data flow restrictions are conditional – that is, the cross-border transfer of personal data is allowed if certain conditions are met. Figure 5 illustrates varieties of data transfer restrictions.

A prominent example of a conditional flow regime is the European Union's GDPR. The 2018 law reinforces and expands individuals' rights with respect to their personal data, including: access to their own data, erasure, portability, and the right to be excluded from automated decision-making (Casalini and González, 2019). The GDPR applies to domestic firms as well as foreign companies that offer goods and services to consumers in the European Union. Transfers of data on European Union individuals to outside of the EU are conditional on recipient country adequacy – meaning the European Data Protection Board determines that the recipient country adequately protects individual data privacy. Absent the adequacy distinction, other safeguards must be in place in the form of binding corporate rules between multinationals and their affiliates, or through the use of standard contractual clauses, which are legal agreements between foreign firms and the EU data protection authorities.

Without a national privacy law, the United States fails to meet the EU adequacy requirement. But EU and US officials reached a workaround solution to allow data transfers. The US–EU Privacy Shield of 2016 allowed US firms to self-certify the adequacy of their privacy safeguards. However, in an example of how the misalignment of national privacy regulations can introduce substantial uncertainty in the legality of cross-border personal data transfers under the GDPR, the European Court of Justice invalidated the agreement in 2020 as a legal mechanism for EU data transfers to the United States. In March 2022, the European Commission and the Biden Administration announced a new framework agreement for transatlantic data transfers, but the specific details of the arrangement have not been determined.

3.2 Data Localization

Data localization laws (sometimes called local storage requirements) require data to be stored on servers located within national borders. While localization is viewed as a separate type of data policy from transfer restrictions, transfer bans amount to de facto local storage and processing (Casalini et al., 2021).

Data localization requirements increase the costs of digital business transactions, since they force firms to establish data centers or contract with cloud computing providers in all countries that have introduced them. When coupled with bans on cross-border data transfers, they impede DVC monetization of data by restricting access to data inputs for analysis. Data localization thus represents one of the most important trade barriers and operating constraints for digital businesses (Hodson, 2019).

Some countries require Internet businesses to establish a local presence, a more onerous requirement than local server mandates. For instance, Turkey's 2020 law[20] and Russia's 2021 Law[21] require foreign Internet companies to establish a local presence, such as a branch or subsidiary.

3.3 Digital Services Taxes

As touched on in Section 2, digitalization enables firms to avoid paying taxes. Aslam and Shah (2021) identify three ways in which the digital economy challenges the existing tax system. First, the Internet facilitates cross-border sales without the need for a physical presence. Second, intangible assets, such as intellectual property, are very easy to transfer across borders but are difficult to value and tax. Third, user data is a significant source of firm value, but user participation is not considered a taxable source of value under the existing international tax system.

There is a lack of international cooperation and consensus on corporate taxes for businesses that sell to markets without a physical presence. Under the current international tax system, multinationals pay corporate income taxes where production occurs. Thus digital services are often untaxed. Several

---

[20] Amendment of the Law on the Regulation of Publications on the Internet and Suppression of Crimes Committed by Means of such Publications.

[21] Federal Law No. 236-FZ on the Internet Activities of Foreign Entities in the Russian Federation.

governments have recently passed new taxes out of a growing frustration with the outsized profits accrued by the tech giants in countries where they have no physical presence.

Digital services taxes are designed to capture additional tax proceeds not covered by the current global tax system. The DSTs are taxes on revenues from the sale of digital services or the digital sale of goods; they apply to residents and foreign suppliers of customers in the country implementing the tax. Digital services taxes are *not* an income (profits) tax or an online sales tax; nor are they a value-added tax. Rather, they are taxes on gross revenues not captured by any treaties. They can cover online sales, digital advertising, e-commerce, data, and streaming.[22]

As of 2022, twenty-nine countries have implemented a DST with rates of 1–15 percent (mean: 7 percent). My accompanying database lists the countries, DST rate, and additional details about the variety of DSTs around the world.

Some governments may impose DSTs in response to declining export competitiveness. Schulze and van der Marel (2021) demonstrate that the early adopters of DSTs in Europe – Italy, Austria, France, UK, and Spain – have experienced a drop in digital services exports over the past fifteen years. The results suggest that the taxes were at least partly motivated by protectionism, in response to rising US imports of digital services.

In 2021, 136 nations agreed to an outline for new global tax rules, and to suspend DSTs for two years, during which time the signatories are required to ratify the agreement. As discussed in Section 2, there is considerable uncertainty at the time of writing regarding whether it will be enacted. The proposal consists of two pillars. Pillar 1 relates to where firms are taxed. It seeks to reallocate the profits of the most profitable digital firms to the countries in which customers and users reside. Under this pillar, 25 percent of profits above a 10 percent profitability margin (defined in excess of revenue) may be taxed in the country in which sales occur. Pillar 2 specifies a global minimum corporate tax rate of 15 percent.[23] The agreement excludes firms in extractive industries and financial services.

The next section presents a political economy framework to explain the variation in digital trade restrictions observed around the world. It argues that the political coalitions around digital trade are likely to differ from traditional coalitions around trade in manufactured goods.

---

[22] www.pwc.com/us/en/services/tax/library/digital-service-taxes.html.

[23] www.oecd.org/tax/beps/statement-on-a-two-pillar-solution-to-address-the-tax-challenges-arising-from-the-digitalisation-of-the-economy-october-2021.htm.

4 Digital Trade Politics

The previous section demonstrated that countries regulate digital trade in very different ways. The United States and Australia have among the loosest cross-border data flow restrictions, while China, Russia, and Vietnam have some of the most stringent restrictions, including the requirement to store personal data in domestic servers. Other countries fall in between these extreme cases. EU member states make cross-border personal data transfers conditional on data privacy protections in the destination country.

Digital trade policies reflect the ways in which countries allocate control rights over data – to firms, to individuals, or to the government. Policy impediments to digital globalization tend to be higher where individuals or governments are the primary arbiters of information, and lower where companies have more control over data. The data governance approaches of the United States, the European Union, and China exemplify three sharply divergent models, and each of these economic powers advocates in favor of its own approach (UNCTAD, 2021; Young, 2022). The United States allocates substantial control over data to private firms, while the European Union favors individual rights. The Chinese model asserts government control over data and information flows.

This section develops a framework to explain variation in data governance through a political economy lens. I build on political economy explanations for trade (and other) policies, which specify the actors that have a stake in the issue, their preferences, and how political institutions shape policymakers' incentives. My theoretical approach does not privilege any single variable in explaining policy variation. Instead, it highlights a multitude of factors that contribute to variation in digital flow restrictions – the influence of firms, workers, and consumers; social norms and values; and political institutions.

Existing models of trade coalitions mainly focus on actors' preferences regarding tariff and nontariff barriers to trade in goods. Some coalitions favor liberalization, while others advocate policy barriers that shield them from global competition. These contending coalitions pressure governments to enact policies that are consistent with their preferences for trade openness or protection (Frieden and Rogowski, 1996; Hiscox, 2001; Kim, 2017; Kim and Milner, 2019; Milner and Kubota, 2005; Osgood, 2018; Rogowski, 1987). Policymakers will respond to these interest group pressures in different ways, depending on the relative political and economic importance of the interest groups, and the incentives generated by political institutions such as elections (Fang and Owen, 2011; Milner and Kubota, 2005; Owen, 2017).

The policy objectives and political influence of businesses anchor most analyses of trade policy coalitions, and they are central to my approach as well. Scholars expect firms to be involved and highly influential in the development of trade policy because it affects the amount of foreign competition in the domestic economy – as well as foreign markets' openness to exports. The potential economic impact of reduced barriers at home and abroad influences firms' support for trade openness. For instance, businesses that import from other countries may benefit from lower trade barriers in their home country, as domestic trade liberalization reduces the costs of imports (Milner, 1988; Osgood et al., 2017). And some firms will benefit from a reduction in barriers abroad that enable export expansion and revenue growth (Baccini et al., 2017). Yet less competitive firms may oppose trade openness because it introduces import competition. As discussed in the previous section, impediments to cross-border digital flows affect businesses' ability to reach new markets, monetize data, and expand abroad. Thus, the framework will focus on examining businesses' likely digital trade policy preferences.

The section explores how the political interests related to digital trade policies line up. To determine who favors digital trade barriers and who opposes them, I consider the social actors that have a strong interest in digital trade policies, their possible policy objectives, and their ability to achieve those objectives by engaging in the political process. Along the way, I assess the ability of prominent theoretical approaches in the political economy of trade to account for the anomalies of digital globalization, especially network advantages and geographic concentration.

Section 4.1 investigates business interests, and includes theoretical discussions of country-level comparative advantage versus firm-level heterogeneity. In Section 4.2, I consider the interests of workers and consumers, whose attitudes toward the privacy aspects of digital trade will influence governments' digital trade policies. In Section 4.3, I examine the stances of civil society actors such as activist groups and nongovernmental organizations (NGOs) – groups that tend to advocate consumer privacy, tax fairness, and economic equity. Since digital globalization ignites concerns linked to all of these issues, it is important to clarify who has a stake and who engages in the political process in an attempt to shape the digital trade policy landscape.

After analyzing the digital trade preferences of various social actors and the possible trade coalitions of actors with shared preferences, in Section 4.4, I examine how different political institutions influence how governments balance the interests of firms and citizens in the development of digital trade policies. Section 4.5 concludes by evaluating the varieties of digital governance.

This section constructs a theoretical framework for examining the political economy of digital globalization. Data limitations and space constraints preclude a detailed examination of the empirical validity of the propositions developed here. The goal is to provide conceptual building blocks and an agenda for future research on digital globalization politics.

4.1 Business Interests

Firms' digital trade interests will depend on their ability to monetize global data flows and benefit from digital trade. Users' inability to own their data (i.e., the lack of property rights over data) means the business that collects the data is able to control, process, and monetize it. Firms in DVCs will seek to extract data from users anywhere they can, and thus will oppose costly impediments such as data localization. Data flow restrictions such as localization increase compliance costs and introduce legal uncertainty around data transfers. The global digital giants thus anchor the digital trade openness coalition, since these firms are best positioned to monetize data (UNCTAD, 2019).

As a result, the largest digital firms will favor data governance that enables their DVCs to expand to as many countries as possible, without restrictions. The economic gains associated with digital globalization will encourage digital giants to oppose restrictions on their ability to access new users, and to collect and transfer data. The objective of the major tech companies is thus quite clear: they strongly oppose tighter controls on the movement of data across borders. Digital giants will lobby against new impediments to digital trade, such as local storage requirements or data flow restrictions.

Given their market dominance, the largest firms have enormous resources to dedicate to their lobbying efforts, which makes them formidable political actors. The tech giants are currently working to embed their favored rules in international agreements so that they can obtain data and users, and forestall domestic efforts at future regulation (Stiglitz, 2019). According to Bank et al. (2021), the tech sector employs 1,452 lobbyists and spends over €97 million (~$115 million) per year lobbying in Europe – more than any other sector (Bank et al., 2021).

Public statements regarding Europe's efforts to exert digital sovereignty, including data localization and flow restrictions, illustrate the tech giants' policy interests. Chris Padilla, IBM's vice president for government and regulatory affairs, stated: "There are some who argue...that data sovereignty is more important than ever. I think what we've seen is that's simply not true. The fact that we've been able to maintain the global economy across borders, with data stored wherever it makes the most sense to store it, shows that data-localization mandates are not the way to go."[24] Google has expressed similar concerns about restrictions on the use of its software, stemming from privacy protections embedded in GDPR. When Austria's data protection authorities declared that Google Analytics did not provide an adequate level of consumer data protection from US national security agencies, Kent Walker, president of global affairs and chief legal officer at Alphabet, wrote: "But Google has offered Analytics-related services to global businesses for more than 15 years and in all that time has never once received the type of demand the Data Protection Authority speculated about. And we don't expect to receive one because such a demand would be unlikely to fall within the narrow scope of the relevant law."[25] From Google's perspective, European regulators overstate a key privacy objection to transatlantic data flows – the risks of surveillance by US authorities.

On the other side of the world, the Chinese approach to controlling information and data has also initiated concerns among US businesses. In a recent American Chamber of Commerce survey, managers called data restrictions the most important obstacle to doing business in China: 76 percent of US firms operating in China reported being concerned about Beijing's policies on data flows and technology security.[26] IBM's Padilla says "the Chinese model is a very different model that is basically built on walling off the internet and creating different national Internets. If we abandon the field, the Chinese are going to push their vision and I don't think that's a vision that is great for the digital economy."[27]

Digital trade openness is also extremely important to companies that engage in the purchase and sale of digital services with other companies. In fact, the vast majority of e-commerce is B2B (Commission, 2017). Cloud services, which include software, infrastructure and platforms are important facilitators of B2B e-commerce. Digital platforms like Alibaba facilitate B2B trade by linking buyers and sellers of bulk orders. Digital value chain firms will oppose policies that increase the costs of their digital B2B transactions.

Consider how the EU Court of Justice's invalidation of the Privacy Shield Framework for transatlantic data flows in 2020 introduced regulatory uncertainty and ignited substantial backlash among affected firms and their trade associations. Negotiations over a replacement framework led to intense lobbying efforts by businesses on both sides of the Atlantic. In 2021, a letter to

---

[24] www.politico.com/newsletters/weekly-trade/2020/09/14/ibms-new-mantra-resist-data-sovereignty-790378 .

[25] http://t.ly/gfqQ9.

[26] https://tinyurl.com/vkd54a3.

[27] www.politico.com/newsletters/weekly-trade/2020/09/14/ibms-new-mantra-resist-data-sovereignty-790378.

US Commerce Secretary Raimondo jointly signed by twenty-four US and EU trade associations stated that "thousands of EU and U.S. companies continue to be impacted by the resulting legal uncertainty for transatlantic data transfers, restrictive interpretations of the ruling risk triggering additional compliance and operational challenges…We urge the U.S. and the EU to swiftly ensure an agreement for secure transatlantic data flows that in turn will strengthen trade, investment, technological cooperation, and reinvigorate the transatlantic partnership."[28] These efforts underscore the costs of policy uncertainty on economic activity and the importance of trade and regulatory agreements to reduce it (Handley and Limão, 2015, 2017).[29]

The policy objectives of firms *competing* with the digital giants are mixed. Looking beyond the dominant US and Chinese firms, there are differences in opinion about digital trade governance. Deducing the objectives of smaller players is complicated because their interests may diverge.

On the one hand, smaller firms could benefit from digital globalization because digital technologies and platforms should enable even the smallest firms to trade goods and services (WTO, 2016).[30] The promise of reaching new markets with a novel app or service, and monetizing new data from outside the country, should reduce support for digital trade restrictions that raise the costs of participating in the global economy.

For instance, studies find that data localization measures, data flow restrictions, and DSTs raise compliance costs, and are particularly onerous for small and medium sized enterprises (SMEs) with limited resources (Burman and Sharma, 2021; Chen et al., 2022; Meltzer, 2019; Sinha and Basu, 2019). Chen et al. (2022) studied how GDPR has affected firm-level performance in sixty-one countries, and found that the negative impact of enhanced data protection on profits was twice as large for small tech companies compared to the full sample. As SMEs seek to enter new jurisdictions abroad, localization mandates may prohibitively raise the costs of entry as well as the costs of transferring data out of the country.[31] The promise of reaching new global customers at low costs through digital channels gives some SMEs economic incentives to join the digital giants in supporting liberalized cross-border digital flows.

---

[28] http://t.ly/WFLA.

[29] In October 2022, President Biden signed an executive order to implement a new EU–US data privacy framework intended to meet the EU adequacy requirement specified in Article 45 of GDPR.

[30] Firms generally need to overcome a certain productivity threshold to afford the fixed costs of selling to foreign markets (Melitz, 2003). The digital economy has lowered these costs, which reduces the productivity threshold for engaging in international trade.

[31] Sinha and Basu (2019) document the policy stances of Indian stakeholders on the issue of data localization.

On the other hand, firms focused on their domestic markets may favor new digital trade barriers that shield from the fierce competition and extractive practices of the digital giants. For example, when data localization emerged as a hot-button issue in India, many domestic businesses supported a legal requirement that foreign firms keep customer data on servers in India. Indian firms have also organized in favor of new DSTs aimed at foreign competitors. Both localization and DSTs would increase the costs of market entry for offshore firms.

Mukesh Ambani, one of India's wealthiest individuals, couched the debate in anti-colonization terms, arguing: "For India to succeed in this data-driven revolution, necessary steps will have to be taken to migrate the control and ownership of Indian data back to India – in other words, Indian wealth back to India. Data colonisation is as bad as the previous forms of colonisation."[32] Ambani and other business leaders favor localization laws that prevent foreign companies from repatriating and monetizing Indian consumers' data. In response, the Indian government passed the Equalization Levy – a 5 percent tax on the Indian revenue of foreign firms with no permanent establishments in the country (commonly called the Google Tax).[33]

For other firms, the variation in their policy stances may not be easily simplified in terms of openness or protectionism. Firms may support some types of restrictions but oppose others. For instance, DSTs uniformly applied to foreign and domestic firms may be less desirable than local server requirements, since the latter tends to raise costs mainly for foreign firms.

To determine whether standard political economy frameworks explain the apparent variation in firms' digital trade policy interests, in the following two subsections I review two prominent approaches to trade politics to assess whether their insights inform the policy interests of firms in the digital economy – those based on *comparative advantage* and those based on *firm-level heterogeneity* in productivity and engagement in international trade.

4.1.1 Factor-Based Comparative Advantage

The economic logic of comparative advantage has traditionally provided powerful insights into trade politics because it explains both the *patterns* of (goods) trade and the distributional *gains* from trade (Hiscox, 2001). The distributional patterns have historically guided our understanding of who would win

---

[32] https://economictimes.indiatimes.com/news/company/corporate-trends/ mukesh-ambani-says-data-colonisation-as-bad-as-physical-colonisation/articleshow/ 67164810.cms.

[33] www.businesstoday.in/current/economy-politics/india-collected-rs-4000-crore-google-tax- since-2016-rs-1100-crore-in-fy20/story/410545.html.

and who would lose from trade openness, which in turn led to straightforward predictions about trade coalitions.

According to the Stolper–Samuelson model, trade liberalization increases the returns for the owners of the relatively abundant factor, whereas incomes fall for the owners of the relatively scarce factor. So in labor-abundant countries like Bangladesh, labor incomes should rise from trade openness, and returns to capital should fall. By contrast, in capital-abundant countries like the United States, capital should gain from trade liberalization whereas labor will lose out (Frieden and Rogowski, 1996; Kim and Milner, 2019; Milner and Kubota, 2005; Rogowski, 1987). Models built around factor-based comparative advantage predict class-based divisions over (goods) trade (Rogowski, 1987). Investigations of their applicability to services are nascent.

Recent research maps the distributional consequences of services trade on firms' policy preferences and lobbying activities (Baccini et al., 2019; Jensen, 2011; Weymouth, 2017). This work anticipates and documents a comparative advantage for the United States in services exports. One implication of these findings is that US services firms will be relatively united in support of services liberalization in the United States and abroad (Baccini et al., 2019). Yet these studies do not consider: (1) how network effects contribute to geographic concentration and market dominance; (2) how data collection imperatives drive preferences for open data flows among the tech giants; or (3) how the extreme market power of a handful of firms in two countries creates defensive, protectionist interests among competing firms in all other countries, including those with factor endowments and technology similar to the United States.

What are some possible implications of comparative advantage for trade in digital products and services? As with manufactured goods, the costs of production should depend on the prices of factors of production and technology. For example, for a platform like Amazon, the costs of the platform service amount to the costs of establishing the website and attracting users; the costs of a marginal transaction on the platform are near zero. That is, the costs of Amazon exporting its platform service consist uniquely of the labor and capital deployed to establish and operate the website in the United States (Deardorff, 2017). We might expect comparative advantage to explain this type of trade just as it would trade in goods (Deardorff, 2017). Capital-intensive tradable services firms in capital-abundant countries like the United States should strongly support the liberalization of services (Baccini et al., 2019), including digital services.

However, two distinguishing features of the digital economy weaken the standard intuition of comparative advantage. The first is *network effects*, which Deardorff (2017) notes:

> Depend less on such factors of production, or even on technology, than on
> the timing of a firm's entry and on the size of the market that they are able
> initially to serve. I suspect that it is no coincidence that the largest platforms
> on the internet today are located in the two largest countries, the United States
> and China, where network effects could provide the greatest benefit. And that
> might well have been true even if some other country – Finland, say, or South
> Korea – had superior factors and technology. (p. 10)

If network effects are more important than factors of production in explaining
the gains from digital trade, then comparative advantage cannot fully account
for the distributional consequences of digital globalization. Instead, the main
beneficiaries are understood to be first-mover firms that are able to accrue
network advantages. Country-level factors of production matter less.

A second complication associated with applying comparative advantage
frameworks to digital trade is that the *data imperative* – not cheap labor –
motivates DVC's global expansion. Manufacturing firms locate (and source
from) abroad to reduce costs. By contrast, digital firms' primary motivation
for international expansion is to capture and extract data from, and sell data-
enhanced services to, new users. Digital firms are not primarily interested in
cheap labor. Instead, they want new consumers and their data because network
effects drive performance and growth. As such, the existing frameworks built
around country endowments of traditional factors of production like labor and
capital are insufficient to explain the variation in digital trade policy stances of
firms around the world.

4.1.2 Firm-Level Heterogeneity

In this section I assess how models anchored in firm-level heterogeneity might
explain variation in digital trade policy stances. These models are grounded in
the observable differences in participation in international trade among firms,
as previous empirical studies have revealed that only a small share of businesses actually engage in trade (Bernard and Jensen, 1999). Trade is generally
conducted, and by volume dominated, by the largest, most productive firms.
These superstar businesses are best able to cover the fixed costs associated
with entering global markets (Bernard et al., 2007; Melitz, 2003; Osgood et al.,
2017). Theoretical approaches based on firm-level differences provide some
insights into digital trade preferences, yet there are notable gaps.

The demonstration of heterogeneity in trade participation led scholars to predict *intra-industry* variation in firms' trade policy stances. One key insight is
that support for trade openness will vary even among firms in the same industry. In particular, the largest, most productive businesses in an industry – those
most likely to export – will favor trade openness (Bailey et al., 1997; Osgood,

2021); whereas smaller, less productive firms will oppose it and seek trade protection in the form of tariffs and nontariff barriers (Kim, 2017; Kim and Milner, 2019; Jensen et al., 2015; Osgood et al., 2017). Firms in global production networks also favor trade liberalization because it lowers the costs of importing intermediate goods (Jensen et al., 2015; Osgood, 2018). Pro-trade coalitions of exporters and importers lobby and offer campaign contributions designed to influence policymakers to support free trade (Baccini et al., 2019; Osgood, 2018, 2021).

At first blush, these firm-level approaches appear to predict the digital trade policy stances of some of the largest digital economy firms quite well. The digital giants are opposed to restrictions on digital trade such as local server requirements and restrictions on data transfers.

However, the largest tech firms sometimes support certain digital regulations. For instance, the tech giants in the US have expressed support for a United States national data privacy law. This stance can be reconciled by the fact that privacy regulations are relatively easy for the largest tech firms to follow, while they can raise fixed costs and thereby potentially exclude smaller competitors from the market. Support for regulation that impedes entry and raises costs for potential competitors is consistent with the theory of regulatory protectionism (Gulotty, 2020).

Outside of China and the United States, where the biggest digital firms are based, the policy stances of even the largest and most productive firms are more varied. As illustrated by the India example discussed above, even some large firms support digital trade barriers, in contradiction to the predictions of heterogeneous firm approaches to trade policy preferences. This trend is probably best understood as defensive posturing for fear that first-mover advantages and network effects have already generated enormous advantages for the digital giants domiciled in the United States and China. The global economic concentration and market dominance of a small number of firms from a small number of countries creates the potential for unique interests and coalitions, unexplained by standard approaches to the political economy of trade.

4.2 Worker and Consumer Interests

The distributional effects of trade can also explain variation in individuals' trade policy preferences. Workers who might expect their wages to grow with trade liberalization should support it, while those in jobs and firms vulnerable to import competition should oppose it.

Factor-based comparative advantage helps explain the distributive effects of trade on workers (Mayda and Rodrik, 2005; Rogowski, 1987; Scheve and

Slaughter, 2001). This framework suggests that education should be correlated with individual support for trade openness, especially in wealthy countries, where lower-skilled workers are at higher risk of displacement through foreign competition. Indeed, trade openness is more popular among higher-skilled individuals (Mayda and Rodrik, 2005; Scheve and Slaughter, 2001; Walter, 2017). Salaries for highly educated workers should increase in the United States as exports in skill-intensive services grow (Baccini et al., 2019; Jensen, 2011; Jensen et al., 2017; Weymouth, 2017).

Others contend that globalization attitudes will differ even among workers within the same industry. Some workers, such as those whose employment involves tasks that can be easily automated or performed in other countries, are at higher risk of job displacement or reduced wages (Blinder and Krueger, 2013; Owen, 2017).[34] In this task-based framework, workers who can be displaced by automation and offshoring are unlikely to support liberalization.

For some people, new products and consumption opportunities are more salient to their globalization attitudes than are employment considerations. Individuals who consume imports and import-competing goods are less likely to support trade protectionism (Baker, 2005), especially if their jobs are less contestable to foreign imports and workers. Yet several features of the digital economy call into question whether traditional economic considerations readily extend to individual attitudes toward digital trade.

For example, the digital economy is not especially labor-intensive, and low-skilled labor is not an important input in DVCs. Moreover, AI and robotics have successfully automated many lower-skilled jobs, especially in manufacturing – employment that had expanded in labor-abundant countries during the GVC era (Baldwin, 2016; Mansfield et al., 2021). Displacement through digital automation is a risk for workers, but much of this automation occurs locally; thus from a policy perspective, it is largely unrelated to trade openness. In capital-rich *industrialized economies*, workers express anxiety over automation and robotization. Yet backlash against digital flows may not be the most natural political expression of this anxiety.[35]

---

[34] Businesses can find workers all over the world without establishing production facilities in each location they choose to hire. Factor costs explain where firms offshore production, but rather than move their entire business abroad, firms might outsource certain stages of production, or even certain tasks, to workers abroad (Grossman and Rossi-Hansberg, 2008). Thus, scholars have scrutinized features of workers' specific occupations – their task compositions and the offshorability of those tasks – to determine whether those workers stand to gain from a globalized economy. This implies that workers in a common industry or skill level – or even those within the same firm – can have very different stances on international trade (Owen, 2017).

[35] On the political salience of automation relative to trade, see Wu (2021), Chaudoin and Mangini (2022), and Hai (2019).

Similarly, open digital markets are unlikely to increase employment opportunities in *labor-abundant* countries. Unlike the increases in employment and wages that many developing countries experienced following the liberalization of goods trade, digital trade openness is unlikely to meaningfully raise worker incomes in labor-abundant countries like Bangladesh since tech platforms are unlikely to establish labor-intensive affiliates there.[36] Thus, there is little reason why lower-skilled workers in poorer countries would support the liberalization of digital trade based on expected wage and employment considerations alone. To the extent that they *do* favor digital openness, it is likely due to their interests as consumers rather than workers.

Most consumer-based accounts of trade politics related to goods tend to highlight that trade liberalization decreases prices and increases product variety. Yet in the digital economy, a focus on prices may be inadequate since many digital services are free.

I contend that two alternative, noneconomic factors will shape peoples' views about digital globalization governance: concerns about (1) privacy and (2) fear of economic or cultural hegemony imparted by the tech giants. Either of these factors could override employment or consumption considerations to explain individuals' support of digital trade, especially if the distributional consequences are not well understood (Rho and Tomz, 2017), or if they offset each other to some degree (e.g., stagnant wages, yet free services). In this section, I consider both alternative explanations in turn and highlight avenues for future research.

First, the concerns related to *privacy* are straightforward. Digital value chains transcend the economic sphere by surveilling individuals and extracting information about them. While digital trade openness increases the variety of services available to consumers, it incurs a (largely noneconomic) cost: unlike goods trade liberalization, which is unambiguously welfare enhancing in the aggregate, digital trade openness entails the erosion of personal privacy. For some, the erosion of personal privacy may offset the welfare gains from openness – such as lower prices and greater product variety – and lead them to oppose certain aspects of digital globalization. So far, widespread backlash to "surveillance capitalism" has not materialized; in what is known as the privacy paradox, individuals' digital behavior belies their stated disquiet over surveillance. Yet privacy concerns continue to rise as people learn more about the growing extent to which algorithms control their behavior (Solove, 2021).

---

[36] An exception might emerge for certain platforms, like Upwork, that enable the long-distance combination of factor inputs for services (Baldwin, 2019).

	Preferred digital trade policy…	
	open	**restricted**
Firms		
Big tech	✓	
DVC firms	✓	
Digital B2B participants	✓	
Domestically focused tech		✓
Individuals		
Consumption-focused	✓	
Privacy advocates		✓
Economic nationalists		✓
Out-group anxious		✓

Figure 6 Anticipated digital trade preferences

Second, prior studies have found that individuals' cultural, racial, and gender identities, and their perceptions of other groups and nations, influence their attitudes toward the trade in goods (Betz et al., 2023; Brutger and Guisinger, 2022; Guisinger, 2017; Hainmueller and Hiscox, 2006; Lü et al., 2012; Mansfield and Mutz, 2009; Mutz, 2021; Mutz and Kim, 2017; Mutz and Lee, 2020). To the extent that these factors also inform consumer preferences about privacy and data security, they might help explain individual views on digital technologies and digital trade openness as well (Girard, 2022; Zhang and Kong, 2021). With the global digital giants centered in the two largest economies, attitudes toward digital globalization may further reflect individual perceptions of the United States and China.

A promising avenue for future research is to investigate how identity and out-group anxieties affect preferences regarding data privacy, digital surveillance, and cross-border information flows. For example, future studies could investigate questions such as: To what extent are individuals concerned about the national origins of popular apps like Instagram or TikTok, and what explains this variation? How do nationalism and out-group anxieties shape individuals' views on geographic concentration in digital markets?[37] And how does the concentration and inequality inherent in the digital economy affect individual perceptions of digital openness?

Figure 6 summarizes the expected digital trade policy preferences of firms and individuals drawn from the analysis.

---

[37] On individual attitudes about antitrust policy.

4.3 Civil Society

Civil society organizations (CSOs) and other nonstate actors play an instrumental role in international policymaking. Transnational civil society can shape digital economy governance through "issue networks" consisting of like-minded actors, which inform policymakers of the preferences of various groups (Price, 1998). Norms are central in the promotion of political and policy change (Finnemore and Sikkink, 1998), and transnational networks of activists have played a central role in diffusing these norms (Keck and Sikkink, 2014). Globally networked activists and CSOs have demonstrated marked success in initiating legislative action on human rights issues (Price, 2003; Risse et al., 1999; Risse and Sikkink, 1999). That advocacy now extends to digital governance (Bennett, 2011; Lehoucq and Tarrow, 2020), including the promotion of new norms related to digital privacy and data governance (Dowd, 2022; Farrell and Newman, 2019b).

Nongovernmental organizations are key civil society actors: they operate independently of business or government, but have the power to influence policy and firms' behavior (Srivastava, 2022). Nongovernmental organizations engage in public debates over digital privacy, regulation, and cross-border data flows in an effort to shape the policy contours of digital globalization. Many of these groups push for stronger public policy protections of consumer rights. Nongovernmental organizations advocating on digital governance often target the economic and political power of Big Tech. A common critique is that tech firms, especially the US giants, exert undue influence over policymakers, which weakens or impedes privacy and other consumer protections.

A letter addressed to the WTO that was signed by 315 international, regional, and national CSOs reveals some of their principal objections to liberalized digital markets.[38] The letter contends that a small number of enormous tech companies have too much power: "nearly all digital trade is dominated by a few global players from the United States and China in ways that are not simply disrupting and re-organizing economic activity but leading to digital domination" (p. 2). It continues by arguing that DVCs are exploitative in their extraction and control of data; that Big Tech's monopoly power constrains the development of local economies; and that digital firms avoid contributing their fair share of taxes.

One objection by CSOs involves the threat of digital imperialism. Groups like Public Citizen, a consumer rights NGO, contend that Big Tech promotes cross-border data flows as a precondition for development in other countries,

---

[38] CSO Letter Against E-Commerce Rules in the WTO.

while in practice, data monetization mainly increases the profits of the largest firms. According to Public Citizen:

> "Quasi monopolistic companies in Europe and America are rushing to connect the next billion people to the internet. But if all the world's data flows in one direction, without restrictions or taxes, this will further reinforce their monopolies over the world's data, widening the privacy gap, and leaving developing countries as consumers or data points, rather than participants in the digital economy" (Kilic and Avila, 2020).

The group's proposed solution to these concerns is "a global standard of privacy and data protection norms" with regulatory measures reflecting those norms: uniform privacy protections and effective enforcement mechanisms (Kilic and Avila, 2020).

Some organizations monitor firms' privacy practices due to what they see as governments' failure to effectively protect consumer privacy. Their goal is to create new norms, standards, and incentives for companies to protect users' rights. One such group, Ranking Digital Rights (RDR), argues that companies are obligated to "be transparent and accountable about how their digital platforms, services, and devices affect users' human rights, especially privacy and expression."[39] It has devised a measure, the RDR Corporate Accountability Index, to quantify companies' disclosed privacy commitments and policies, based on international human rights standards.

4.4 Domestic Political Institutions

Governments face complicated questions about how to govern and regulate the digital economy. Digital trade policies reflect the interests of policymakers and the governance institutions in place. Policymakers face trade-offs between building consumer trust and protecting individual data privacy, while also facilitating a competitive digital economy. They must decide how to assign ownership over data, and whether to restrict cross-border data flows.

The privacy–innovation tradeoff confounds attempts to define an optimal privacy protection regime. There is clearly a tension between protecting personal privacy and encouraging technological innovations that may emerge from the use of data. Digital value chain innovations can increase consumer welfare and economic productivity, providing new services at lower prices. Overly strict privacy regulations may make economies of scale difficult to achieve, which will hamper innovation and may slow productivity and reduce product quality.

---

[39] https://rankingdigitalrights.org/about/.

The nature of governments' policy responses to cross-border data flows reflects the constraints that the domestic political system imposes on policymakers. Where democratic institutions such as competitive elections and independent courts constrain leaders, digital trade policies tend to reflect business and voter concerns about the economic and social consequences of the digital economy, which include data privacy, rising economic consolidation and inequality, and citizens' aversion to multinational tax avoidance strategies.

Citizen concerns about digital globalization raise questions about its political sustainability in the absence of international coordination and cooperation. This is because cross-national information and data flows, a defining feature of digital globalization, are incompatible with key tenets of capitalist democracies: digital globalization can erode individual rights (including property rights, anti-discrimination, and privacy) and foster concentrated markets dominated by monopolies. These exigencies have led to government policy responses designed to restrain data and information flows.

Thus far I have highlighted sources of division over digital trade policies among businesses, voters, and civil society – political pressures to which democratic governments tend to respond.

Autocratic governments have different political motivations for digital governance. Because they are not held accountable in competitive elections or constrained by independent judiciaries, autocrats are shielded to some degree from citizen backlash to market concentration or tax avoidance; citizens have few mechanisms with which to sanction policymakers for anticompetitive market outcomes. And in general, such regimes place less emphasis on individual liberty.

For autocrats, digital surveillance can provide intelligence that enables more targeted forms of repression. Autocrats are more likely to restrict potentially destabilizing information flows and to adopt surveillance technologies to identify potential dissidents (Deibert and Rohozinski, 2010; Dragu and Lupu, 2021; King et al., 2013; Roberts, 2018), while restrictions on Internet accessibility make it harder for opposition factions to organize (Gohdes, 2014, 2020). Authoritarian regimes increasingly employ AI tools like facial recognition to identify and suppress opposition and dissent (Dragu and Lupu, 2021). China's ability to produce and deploy inexpensive surveillance technology has promoted their use in other authoritarian countries (Andersen, 2020; Weiss, 2019), and served to export aspects of China's approach to digital governance (Erie and Streinz, 2021).

Autocrats' efforts to control and monitor information flows often include policies like data flow restrictions and data localization requirements. Saudi Arabia's National Data Governance Interim Regulations of 2020 require

storage and local processing within Saudi Arabia "in order to ensure pres-
ervation of the digital national sovereignty over such data."[40] Russia's 2021
Federal Law No. 236-FZ on the Internet Activities of Foreign Entities requires
establishment of a local presence for foreign Internet companies for activities
focused on Russian users. Algeria's NR 18-07 law requires that e-commerce
platforms host websites from data centers located in Algeria. The Chinese
government demands access to consumer data, and companies are required
to comply. China's Cybersecurity Law of 2017 compels private businesses to
share consumer data with government security services. The law also allows
Chinese authorities to access data from foreign firms operating in China.

Autocrats are also adept at forcing foreign firms to transfer technology or
enter joint ventures in exchange for market access. To access the Chinese
market, US corporations are engaged in joint ventures and controversial maneu-
vers. For instance, to avoid legal repercussions in the United States and to
appease the Chinese authorities, Apple ceded ownership of its Chinese user
data to a Chinese government-owned company (Liu, 2021). Apple also blocks
apps that it believes will upset Chinese officials.[41] In general, China's restrictive approach to digital governance requires a difficult adjustment for foreign
firms operating there (Gao, 2018).

But this variation in digital governance cannot be attributed solely to a
simplistic democracy versus authoritarian dichotomy. Autocrats attempt to har-
ness the economic benefits of the digital economy, and they work to shield
themselves from political pressures stemming from DVC activities. China
aggressively promoted the growth of its tech sector, in part to "outsource"
the development of market-promoting institutions such as contracting rights
in the absence of an independent judiciary (Liu, 2022). The Chinese government recently initiated a strong regulatory pushback against some of the
major players in its tech sector, including the Personal Information Protection
Law (PIPL) of 2021. The PIPL requires that firms collecting personal information obtain the express consent of the individual. Such consent "must be
informed, freely given, demonstrated by a clear action of the individual, and
may later be withdrawn."[42] The PIPL also requires that entities processing personal data store that information locally. These developments demonstrate a
responsiveness to societal and political pressures related to private sector digital
surveillance, rising inequality, and the economic power of the technology jug-
gernauts. Authoritarian governments are not immune to the social and political
externalities of digital globalization discussed here.

---

[40] www.albrightstonebridge.com/news/asg-analysis-saudi-arabia-publishes-national-data-gover
nance-interim-regulations.
[41] https://tinyurl.com/3bdxuf28.
[42] https://tinyurl.com/2p9xstxs.

4.5 Varieties of Digital Governance

There is a general consensus that three main digital governance models have emerged around the world, exemplified by the differing approaches of the European Union, China, and the United States (Aaronson and Leblond, 2018; Chander and Schwartz, 2022; Ferracane and van der Marel, 2021; UNCTAD, 2021; World Bank, 2021; Young, 2022). They differ based on whose control over personal data is privileged: individuals, the government, or business.

The *activist* approach views personal data privacy as a fundamental right and privileges individual control over data. The activist approach thus reflects the interests of privacy advocates, and the stated preferences of CSOs concerned about the economic and political power of Big Tech.

The European Union is an archetype of the activist approach. The European Union passed the GDPR to confront the erosion of digital privacy. This law sets out a conditional data transfer approach: international transfers of citizen data are only allowed if the EU data protection authorities have determined in advance that the receiving country or firm offers adequate data privacy protections (World Bank, 2021). Regulators enforce the adequacy requirement through binding corporate rules, standard contractual clauses, data subject consent, and other codes of conduct (Ferracane and van der Marel, 2021). The emphasis on personal data protection is partly motivated by the belief that protection will build trust between consumers and companies (Aaronson and Leblond, 2018). The activist model is diffusing as other countries seek to meet the European Union's adequacy requirement. The European Commission has recognized Andorra, Argentina, Canada, Israel, Japan, New Zealand, the Republic of Korea, Switzerland, the United Kingdom, and Uruguay as providing adequate protection.[43]

In addition to data privacy, the EU competition authority has taken an activist stance against the digital giants' anticompetitive practices. The European Union has led on pursuing an agreement on multinational corporation (MNC) taxation, and threatens to enact digital taxes targeting US tech companies, encouraging the United States to cooperate on a G7 framework agreement for MNC taxation.

The *restrictionist* approach makes the state the most powerful arbiter of data. This model allows government authorities to override individuals' rights to personal privacy (Ferracane and van der Marel, 2021). Governments may follow the restrictionist model in pursuit of multiple objectives. In some countries, data flow restrictions are designed to buffer local firms from the digital giants

---

[43] See the European Commission Adequacy Decisions.

in order to build up national digital champions. In this way, the model reflects the interests of domestically oriented firms. Another goal is to control information in efforts to solidify the power of the ruling party, often under the guise of protecting national security or public order.

Countries following the restrictionist approach place limits on all sorts of data transfers and digital transactions. For example, China, Nigeria, Russia, and Vietnam limit access to their domestic markets by placing high barriers on digital services. They also restrict aspects of cross-border data transfers, and require copies of certain types of personal data to be stored domestically (World Bank, 2021). Some countries, like China, Congo, and Egypt also restrict domestic information flows, for example by imposing extensive government access to or control over data (Aaronson and Leblond, 2018; Ferracane and van der Marel, 2021), and by intermittently shutting down the Internet to all or certain parts of the country.[44]

A third path, the *laissez-faire* approach, confers control over data to firms. Countries pursuing this approach allow businesses to control and monetize personal data with few restrictions. Countries like the United States permit open cross-border flows of data with limited government restrictions (Aaronson and Leblond, 2018; World Bank, 2021). Under this approach, countries use trade agreements to ban data localization and restrictions on cross-border data flows. The motive is to develop economies of scale and scope to reap the benefits of competitive advantage in digital services (Aaronson and Leblond, 2018). Ultimately, the objectives of this approach are innovation and growth of the tech sector, with the benefits of consumer choice, lower prices, and greater product variety. This model reflects the interests of domestic firms in globally integrated DVCs, including Big Tech and digital B2B participants.

The political sustainability of the laissez-faire approach is highly uncertain. The hope may be that the market will prevent firms from overstepping privacy norms, and that companies will self-regulate.[45] Countries following the laissez-faire model have done little to address the erosion of privacy or the weakening of market competition that digital globalization entails. Rising industry concentration and tech privacy overreach draw criticism and heightened scrutiny (Stoller, 2019; Wu, 2020; Zuboff, 2019). Yet policymakers have thus far bet that consumers prefer the services that digital globalization offers more than they oppose the downsides.

---

[44] Government have shut down portions of the Internet recently in Bangladesh, Democratic Republic of Congo, Egypt, Indonesia, Iran, Iraq, Sudan, Myanmar, and Zimbabwe. Even democratic India shut down the Internet for a short period in 2020 (Source: www.hrw.org/world-report/2020/country-chapters/global-5#).

[45] On the political logic of self-regulation, see Malhotra et al. (2019).

5 Institutional Prerequisites for Digital Globalization

The preceding sections have explored the political implications of a new form of global economic production. Digital value chains use data as a central input in their production process. Yet unlike other inputs, there are no global rules defining property rights over data. Without property rights and meaningful constraints on firms' ability to collect and monetize data, the global digital economy has rapidly concentrated, allowing a small number of firms to amass enormous economic power. The political fault lines include concerns about individual privacy, market concentration and inequality, and MNC tax avoidance facilitated by intangibles. In response, many governments have pursued ad hoc policy impediments to cross-border digital commerce. The risk is that these impediments lead to an increasingly siloed global digital economy.

This section examines the global politics of the digital economy. I consider the policy prerequisites for digital market integration, and argue that global economic cooperation in the digital era will require building consensus around data privacy, market competition, and taxation. Before coordinated *liberalization* of cross-border data flows, a politically sustainable digital globalization requires coordinated *regulation*.

5.1 Digital Globalization Paradox

The politics of digital globalization are rooted in the lack of property rights over its central input, data. Controversies arise because the global digital economy lacks governance institutions to mediate exchanges in data and data-driven services. This has led DVCs to expand and large digital firms to emerge through the extraction and monetization of data, and by using intangibles to evade taxes. Here I briefly review the three main ways in which digital globalization threatens individual rights and the functioning of competitive markets, two hallmarks of capitalist democracies. I then demonstrate the prerequisites for a politically sustainable integration of national digital economies through the digital globalization paradox.

Individual privacy. Individuals' digital footprints include data revealing the most intimate aspects of their lives. The DVC, the engine behind digital globalization, requires the intensive use of personal data as an input to the production of new products and services, which entail constant transfers of data across national borders.

Concentration and monopoly. Economies of scale and scope, first-mover advantages, and tax avoidance lead to monopoly positions, anticompetitive practices, and market concentration. Digital platforms facilitate anticompetitive practices, such as the abuse of dominance and predatory pricing.

Tax avoidance. Digital technologies facilitate tax avoidance via profit shifting and transactions involving intangibles. They also facilitate sales of digital services, many of which are untaxed because the antiquated global corporate tax system based on the location of production. MNC tax avoidance strategies shift the tax burden from capital to labor (Rodrik, 2011; Zucman, 2015).

These politically contentious features of digital globalization force states to confront trade-offs. Open digital markets unleash valuable digital services to consumers, often at zero monetary cost. Yet the DVCs that produce digital services surveil consumers, extract data resources, and often pay little in taxes. The leading firms dominate their markets, and their market power engenders undue political influence (Callander et al., 2021). There is a strong tension between digital globalization on the one hand, and individual rights and market competition on the other.

The trade-offs lead governments toward different approaches to digital trade governance. One strategy is to ignore the consequences of digital globalization for individual rights and competitive markets. This strategy can facilitate the development of the domestic tech sector, but it risks a backlash among citizens, as well as policy conflict with other nations. Another strategy is to restrict digital globalization through ad hoc measures such as data transfer restrictions and data localization measures. These policy instruments may enhance citizens' digital privacy. But if pursued in an uncoordinated manner, such ad hoc arrangements will lead to the stratification and splintering of digital markets, which can slow the growth of the digital economy.

Consider how these trade-offs manifest in the real world. The European Union privileges consumer data privacy and attempts to control data from flowing out of the European Union – meaning it aspires to digital sovereignty and the protection of consumer rights, a digital governance model called the *activist* approach. But Europe's tech sector lags behind that of the United States and China. The United States is home to a dominant tech sector and open data flows: it does not pursue digital sovereignty. But it is unable to commit to consumer data privacy and industrial concentration is high, consistent with the *laissez-faire* approach. China's tech sector is competitive and growing, and its government famously restricts data and other information flows, but Chinese consumers are constantly surveilled by businesses and the state. In China's quest for tech dominance and control over information, personal privacy is largely unaddressed, as the government is the ultimate arbiter of data rights. China exemplifies the *restrictionist* approach to digital governance.

Divergent governance models threaten digital globalization. The politically contentious exigencies of the digital economy create incentives for governments to control data flows and restrict cross-border digital transactions. This impetus will continue as long as the contentious issues (privacy, concentration, and taxation) remain unaddressed. Under the most dire scenarios, global digital markets could splinter entirely, resulting in digital silos (Aaronson and Leblond, 2018; Chander and Schwartz, 2022). What can be done to avoid this outcome?

To generate the domestic political support for digital market integration, countries will first need to agree to two sets of rules. I call these rules the institutional foundations for digital globalization.

One, integration that respects consumers' rights requires countries to agree on a baseline level of consumer data privacy protection. Without regulatory cooperation on privacy, governments with strong domestic privacy laws and norms are likely to restrict data exports and require some data to be localized (Meltzer, 2019). Domestic regulators need to be confident that their domestic regulatory goals will not be violated once data leaves their jurisdiction; this can only be achieved if countries harmonize their approaches to privacy regulation.

Two, domestic political buy-in for digital globalization also requires some semblance of market competition and tax fairness. Network advantages and lax regulation have led to industries dominated by a handful of firms. Meanwhile, digital firms have avoided paying a proportional share of taxes due to an antiquated tax system premised on physical production. From the vantage point of most governments, US and Chinese firms extract data resources that fuel an insurmountable competitive advantage relative to domestic firms. A combination of anticompetitive practices, from abuse of dominance to intellectual property theft, sparks political backlash from which ad hoc digital trade impediments arise. Support for digital market openness, and the rollback of digital trade restrictions, therefore requires agreements on taxation and competition policy.

This regulatory convergence requirement represents a **digital globalization paradox**. For digital economies to integrate without political backlash, countries must build a common set of institutional foundations that constrain the activities of the most dominant digital firms. For digital globalization to achieve sustainable public support, it will require some convergence on policies for which cooperation has no precedent. Paradoxically, for digital globalization to flourish, the multinationals that currently dominate digital markets must first be restrained.

Digital globalization requires countries to align on regulatory matters that fall outside of traditional trade policies. Digital globalization is inherently incompatible with individual privacy and competitive markets; thus it is politically unsustainable without new institutions to protect individual privacy rights and preserve market competition. Agreements on privacy protections, antitrust,

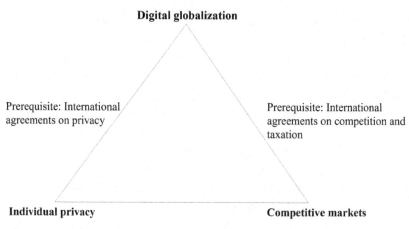

Digital globalization

Prerequisite: International
agreements on privacy

Prerequisite: International
agreements on competition and
taxation

Individual privacy   **Competitive markets**

Figure 7 Institutional foundations for digital globalization

and taxation are needed to overcome the politically problematic features of the digital economy. Individual governments cannot overcome the incompatibilities alone: digital globalization requires policy coordination. Figure 7 illustrates the institutional prerequisites to a politically sustainable digital globalization.

A new globalization paradigm arises from the unique features of data and the activities of DVCs. In the previous era of globalization, market integration mainly required coordinated *liberalization* – of tariffs primarily, but also of barriers to international investment. In the current era, coordinated liberalization will not suffice. To build the political and policy foundations for digital economies to expand and integrate, DVCs must first be constrained through coordinated *regulation* across countries.

My framework points to a number of possible medium-term scenarios for the governance of the digital economy. Building issue linkages has been shown to overcome domestic political opposition (Davis, 2004), but the task becomes much more complex with the range of regulatory incongruities, political institutions, and domestic policy interests at play.

One possibility is that no new multilateral policy foundations for the digital economy are constructed. Rather, countries continue to pursue versions of digital sovereignty, and control of information flows across borders. Without a multilateral agreement on taxation, countries pursue ad hoc DSTs. Barriers to data and information, bans of foreign platform firms, and data flow restrictions will continue to increase. Digital globalization will stall, and firms will be forced to navigate a web of compliance requirements to sell digital services abroad.

In another possible scenario, democratic politics forces leaders to coordinate on privacy policy, since regulatory divergence will become untenable: national governments' promises to protect citizen data are meaningless if they are unable to ensure that other countries will follow suit.[46] I exclude autocratic countries from this scenario for a reason. We characterize autocrats by their unwillingness to extend basic human rights, including the right to privacy, to their citizens. The autocratic state's deployment of digital surveillance to tamp down on citizens' potential unrest entails violations of privacy, often facilitated by data sharing between private firms and the state. It is therefore highly unlikely that autocratic regimes will agree to meaningful privacy reforms that constrain firms' or governments' ability to collect and process private information.

A somewhat less likely scenario is that countries coordinate over competition policy to some degree. The continuation of economic dominance by the largest tech platforms is politically unappealing; coordination over a more strident competition policy can help ensure that value created in DVCs is more equitably shared between businesses and consumers. Yet competition rules are deeply embedded in national political economies (Hall and Soskice, 2001), and convergence over these rules would encounter fierce resistance from powerful firms (Weymouth, 2016). As an illustration of the complexities involved in a multilateral approaches to competition consider that in 1997, the WTO named competition policy an important issue and set up a working group to explore its relationship to international trade and investment. Seven years later, the working group was dismantled after failing to develop a multilateral framework.

Another possibility involves a global agreement on taxation. It is politically damaging for states to allow MNCs to avoid taxation in jurisdictions in which they sell and amass large market shares. Citizens are increasingly perturbed by MNC tax avoidance; thus, leaders may be forced to develop a global solution. Progress through the OECD was announced in 2021, as 134 countries agreed in principle to a global minimum rate and greater leverage to tax digital services. As of this writing, the consummation of that deal remains highly uncertain, in no small part because the US Congress has not passed the reform necessary to comply. Poland and Hungary are among the countries that have moved to block the agreement. A meaningful agreement requires near-universal compliance, since countries that deviate from an agreement can quickly become tax havens, nullifying the intent of the agreement.

---

[46] On the prospects for a global privacy agreement, see Chander and Schwartz (2022).

5.2 Implications for Global Economic Cooperation

What body should spearhead agreements on digital trade, taxes, competition, and privacy? International institutions mediate economic relations between states, but there is no international body currently setting the global rules for digital commerce. The WTO was initially established to set and enforce rules for trade in *goods*, not services. Yet most restrictions on digital trade are regulatory measures affecting market access, services, and data flows, rather than tariffs.

The WTO covers some regulatory policies that underpin services trade (Casalini et al., 2021), but past agreements have not been updated to address new forms of digital trade (Bacchus, 2022; Wu, 2017). For instance, the GATS is relevant to some aspects of digital services transactions, but the agreement was concluded decades ago, when digital trade in services was nascent. The GATS categorizes services using an antiquated system that cannot account for the types of digitally delivered services that exist today. For example, data flows over the Internet enable additive manufacturing, which has no classification under the GATS W/120 scheme (Azmeh et al., 2020). There is thus a pressing need to update WTO rules and norms to govern digital trade, but the challenge is stark given the lack of US leadership (Bowen and Broz, 2021) and the challenges posed by China's unique economic system (Weiss and Wallace, 2021; Wu, 2016, 2019).

It is unclear whether existing WTO rules proscribe specific policy impediments to digital trade, such as data flow restrictions or localization measures. Some GATS disciplines may bar measures that explicitly discriminate against services exporters from abroad, and those that restrict market access in sectors for which countries have made commitments under the GATS. Yet to date, no WTO panel has explicitly considered the legality of data localization measures under the GATS. The lack of explicit rules or prior rulings generates significant uncertainty about how disputes would be resolved (Hodson, 2019).

Previous rulings provide some guidance on how GATS commitments might be interpreted in the context of technological advances in services delivery. The WTO Appellate Body ruling *DS285 US-Gambling*[47] established that the manner of service delivery was technologically neutral, meaning that a commitment to liberalize cross-border trade in services applies to any technological means of delivery of that service. In other words, services commitments under the GATS may apply to services supplied through digital means (Hodson, 2019).

Yet there are disagreements over whether GATS commitments cover *new* digital services such as cloud computing or 3D printing (Meltzer, 2019). The

---

[47] www.wto.org/english/tratop_e/dispu_e/cases_e/ds285_e.htm.

WTO has not established whether technological neutrality of delivery means that these new services can simply be mapped to arcane industry classifications, which were developed in the early days of the Internet. Advances in digital technologies that were not contemplated at the time, or captured in older industry classifications, reveal a host of ambiguities concerning what is covered and what is not.[48]

The general consensus is that international rules for digital trade need to be established, and that the WTO is late to the game. Recently, a group of eighty-six WTO members began discussions under a Joint Statement Initiative on trade-related aspects of electronic commerce. The discussions incorporate a broad set of issues, including privacy and transparency (Casalini et al., 2021). A further concern is that the WTO is not presently able to govern the regulatory aspects of digital trade, let alone complicated "nontrade" issues like privacy, competition policy, and taxation. The rules need updating, but a rewriting requires coordination on complicated regulatory issues; trade forums might be inadequate (Ahmed, 2019; Cowhey and Aronson, 2017; Meltzer, 2019).

In the absence of multilateral arrangements, countries have used preferential trade agreements (PTAs) to develop rules for new products and to engender political support (Baccini and Dür, 2012; Davis, 2009; Wu, 2017). The digital issues most commonly covered in preferential agreements relate to e-commerce (Burri and Polanco, 2020). Preferential trade agreements differ in their level of commitment to provisions protecting personal data privacy and taxes on digital transactions (Casalini et al., 2021). Since 2008, twenty-nine trade agreements among seventy-two countries have included provisions on data flows (Casalini et al., 2021). As of 2020, nineteen jurisdictions explicitly bar requirements to locate servers within the trade partner country (Nemoto and Lopez Gonzalez, 2021).

Privacy agreements may emerge through coordination within some sets of plurilateral trade pacts, as well as through agreements on regulatory principles, rather than fully fledged trade accords. Private regulatory arrangements are one possible avenue (Büthe and Mattli, 2011). Another involves "hybrid institutions," in which states create frameworks of rules that are implemented by firms (Farrell, 2003). The (now defunct) Safe Harbor and Privacy Shield agreements, and efforts related to their replacement, are examples of efforts to piece together transatlantic coordination through hybrid institutions. In principle, hybrids can bridge incongruous domestic regulations in different states, but only if the agreed framework conforms with domestic law.

---

[48] Most WTO members' GATS commitments followed UN Provisional Central Product Classification codes, which were finalized in 1991.

Collaboration among like-minded domestic regulatory authorities may contribute to international cooperation on digital governance. Examining Europe's privacy frameworks prior to the GDPR, Newman (2008a; 2008b) highlights the role of transgovernmental policy entrepreneurs – national data privacy authorities that collaborated to define the supranational privacy agenda that led to Europe's 1995 data privacy directive. This directive required member states to enact similar provisions on the governance of personal information, and mandated the creation of data privacy enforcement authorities.

Ultimately, democratic governments share incentives to coordinate on a common set of rules. There is widespread agreement among Western democracies on the need to resist a more authoritarian approach. Europe has been a vocal advocate of shared rules. Jeppe Kofod, Denmark's foreign minister, commented, "We need to build alliances with like-minded countries. Societies that are concerned about protecting democratic principles. Right now, we don't have a clear external policy."[49] US Senator Mark Warner called for greater cooperation between the United States and the European Union on digital governance, saying, "This is the defining economic issue of our time. There needs to be a sense of urgency...that's what's needed to speed up the West's response to China."[50] The devil is in the details, of course. A central debate concerns how to regulate and tax Big Tech. "Tech giants need to meet their societal obligations," added Kofod, signaling continued EU–US divisions emanating from the dominance of US tech giants.

Though this Element has focused on the economic aspects of digital globalization, geopolitical and national security considerations related to digital technologies will also hinder further cooperation. The US–China relationship is central, of course (Young, 2022). China's ambitious plans for technological superiority threaten US interests. Bipartisan warnings by US policymakers about China's potential use of 5G for espionage or sabotage demonstrated deep discord emanating from competing economic models, mutual distrust, and competitiveness concerns.[51] They also reveal broader fears that China's technological rise threatens US security and alters the balance of power.

Economic and security considerations are increasingly intertwined. States can leverage economic networks to coerce other states by imposing costs on others if they have political authority over the international networked structures through which information travels (Farrell and Newman, 2019a). Since

---

[49] www.politico.eu/newsletter/digital-bridge/digital-geopolitics-frances-haugen-climate-misinformation/.

[50] www.politico.eu/article/mark-warner-digital-bridge-tech-china/.

[51] www.theverge.com/2019/3/17/18264283/huawei-security-threat-experts-china-spying-5g.

the digital giants are concentrated in the United States and China, the potential for coercion by these countries cannot be overlooked. As Farrell and Newman (2019a) explain, coercion can be applied to gather information and compel policy change. In such an environment, agreement on new rules for digital trade may require a coordinated approach among smaller states to act as a bulwark against larger, more powerful actors like the United States and China. In some instances, privacy laws may partially defang the most powerful actors by limiting the types and amount of data that can be collected.

5.3 Future Research

This Element has developed an analytic framework for studying the politics of digital globalization. I analyzed the new sources of political friction that digital globalization represents, and examined the new types of policy barriers to international information flows that governments have introduced. I then presented a theoretical framework for explaining policy variation across countries. This final section has argued that international cooperation on digital governance requires a set of regulatory foundations upon which countries will need to coordinate. These contributions represent a starting point; much work remains. In conclusion, I highlight four topics and issues for future research.

First, the lack of property rights over data is central to the politics of digital globalization. Consumer data privacy concerns stem from consumers' inability to control their data. Political battles over the control of personal information are just beginning. Future work should assess consumer attitudes to personal data: to what extent do individuals value privacy, and what explains variation in individual preferences for privacy around the world?

Second, a small number of very large firms dominates the digital economy. Their rise coincides with widening inequalities of income and wealth in many countries. Yet some of the largest and most powerful companies provide many services at no monetary cost: they barter services for user data. How politically sustainable is this exchange? Do large corporations face a political backlash? Do attitudes toward the tech giants drive a new antitrust activism? Voters' attitudes will ultimately influence policy, so understanding the mass politics of industry concentration and inequality will be important.

Third, governments are imposing new types of policy barriers to digital trade and information flows across borders. Linking trade barriers to political interests has been a fruitful line of research in international relations. We know a lot about the political pressures that lead governments to pursue barriers to trade in goods, but much less about the political motivations behind services and digital trade restrictions. It will also be important to study the effects of digital trade restrictions on economic activity: who are the main winners and losers from these policies?

Finally, I have argued here that international cooperation on privacy, competition, and taxation are prerequisites – the policy foundations – for a politically sustainable digital globalization. We do not yet understand what types of institutions would be required to successfully achieve international cooperation on these issues. Future theoretical work should examine the political incentives and institutional structures that would facilitate multilateral cooperation on digital governance. The integration of the global digital economy is a political process. The success or failure of that process will determine the nature of international economic relations for the rest of the century.

References

Aaronson, S. A. (2021). The Difficult Past and Troubled Future of Digital Protectionism. In Borchert, I. and Winters, L. A., editors, *Addressing Impediments to Digital Trade*, 141–168. CEPR Press.

Aaronson, S. A. and Leblond, P. (2018). Another Digital Divide: The Rise of Data Realms and its Implications for the WTO. *Journal of International Economic Law*, 21(2):245–272.

Acemoglu, D. and Restrepo, P. (2019). Automation and New Tasks: How Technology Displaces and Reinstates Labor. *Journal of Economic Perspectives*, 33(2):3–30.

Agrawal, A., Gans, J., and Goldfarb, A. (2018a). Economic Policy for Artificial Intelligence. *Innovation Policy and the Economy*, 19:139–159.

Agrawal, A., Gans, J., and Goldfarb, A. (2018b). *Prediction Machines: The Simple Economics of Artificial Intelligence.* Harvard Business Press.

Agrawal, A., Gans, J. S., and Goldfarb, A. (2019). Artificial Intelligence: The Ambiguous Labor Market Impact of Automating Prediction. *Journal of Economic Perspectives*, 33(2):31–50.

Ahlquist, J., Copelovitch, M., and Walter, S. (2020). The Political Consequences of External Economic Shocks: Evidence from Poland. *American Journal of Political Science*, 64(4):904–920.

Ahmed, U. (2019). The Importance of Cross-border Regulatory Cooperation in an Era of Digital Trade. *World Trade Review*, 18(S1):S99–S120.

Andersen, R. (2020). The Panopticon is Already Here. *The Atlantic*. www.theatlantic.com/magazine/archive/2020/09/china-ai-surveillance/6 14197/.

Ansolabehere, S., De Figueiredo, J. M., and Snyder Jr., J. M. (2003). Why is There so Little Money in US Politics? *Journal of Economic Perspectives*, 17(1):105–130.

Arrow, K. J. (1962). Economic Welfare and the Allocation of Resource for Inventions, In R. R. Nelson, editor, *The Rate and Direction of Inventive Activity: Economic and Social Factors*. 609–626. Princeton University Press.

Aslam, A. and Shah, A. (2021). Taxing the Digital Economy. In R. De Mooij, A. Klemm, and V. Perry, editors, *Corporate Income Taxes under Pressure. Why Reform Is Needed and How It Could Be Designed*, 189–226. International Monetary Fund.

Avila Pinto, R. (2018). Digital Sovereignty or Digital Colonialism: The Sur File on Internet and Democracy. *Sur - International Journal on Human Rights*, 27:15–28.

Azmeh, S., Foster, C., and Echavarri, J. (2020). The International Trade Regime and the Quest for Free Digital Trade. *International Studies Review*, 22(3):671–692.

Bacchus, J. (2022). *Trade Links: New Rules for a New World*. Cambridge University Press.

Baccini, L. and Dür, A. (2012). The New Regionalism and Policy Interdependence. *British Journal of Political Science*, 42(1):57–79.

Baccini, L., Osgood, I., and Weymouth, S. (2019). The Service Economy: US Trade Coalitions in an Era of Deindustrialization. *The Review of International Organizations*, 14(2):261–296.

Baccini, L., Pinto, P. M., and Weymouth, S. (2017). The Distributional Consequences of Preferential Trade Liberalization: Firm-level Evidence. *International Organization*, 71(2):373–395.

Baccini, L. and Weymouth, S. (2021). Gone for Good: Deindustrialization, White Voter Backlash, and US Presidential Voting. *American Political Science Review*, 115(2):550–567.

Bailey, M. A., Goldstein, J., and Weingast, B. R. (1997). The Institutional Roots of American Trade Policy: Politics, Coalitions, and International Trade. *World Politics*, 49(3):309–338.

Baker, A. (2005). Who Wants to Globalize? Consumer Tastes and Labor Markets in a Theory of Trade Policy Beliefs. *American Journal of Political Science*, 49(4):924–938.

Baldwin, R. (2016). *The Great Convergence*. Harvard University Press.

Baldwin, R. (2019). *The Globotics Upheaval: Globalization, Robotics, and the Future of Work*, Oxford University Press

Ballard-Rosa, C., Malik, M. A., Rickard, S. J., and Scheve, K. (2021). The Economic Origins of Authoritarian Values: Evidence from Local Trade Shocks in the United Kingdom. *Comparative Political Studies*, 54(13):2321–2353.

Bank, M., Duffy, F., Leyendecker, V., and Silva, M. (2021). The Lobby Network - Big Tech's Web of Influence in the EU.Corporate Europe Observatory.

Bennett, C. J. (2011). Privacy Advocacy from the Inside and the Outside: Implications for the Politics of Personal Data Protection in Networked Societies. *Journal of Comparative Policy Analysis: Research and Practice*, 13(2):125–141.

Bernard, A. B. and Jensen, J. B. (1999). Exceptional Exporter Performance: Cause, Effect, or Both? *Journal of International Economics*, 47(1):1–25.

Bernard, A. B., Jensen, J. B., Redding, S. J., and Schott, P. K. (2007). Firms in International Trade. *Journal of Economic Perspectives*, 21(3):105–130.

Betz, T., Fortunato, D., and O'Brien, D. Z. (2023). Do Women Make More Protectionist Trade Policy? *American Political Science Review*.

Blinder, A. S. and Krueger, A. B. (2013). Alternative Measures of Offshorability: A Survey Approach. *Journal of Labor Economics*, 31(S1):S97–S128.

Boix, C. (2019). *Democratic Capitalism at the Crossroads*. Princeton University Press.

Borchert, I. and Winters, L. A. (2021). *Addressing Impediments to Digital Trade*. CEPR Press.

Bowen, T. R. and Broz, J. L. (2021). The Domestic Political-Economy of the WTO Crisis: Lessons for Preserving Multilateralism. *Global Perspectives*, 3(1): 1–20.

Branstetter, L. G., Glennon, B., and Jensen, J. B. (2019). The IT Revolution and the Globalization of R&D. *Innovation Policy and the Economy*, 19(1):1–37.

Broz, J. L., Frieden, J., and Weymouth, S. (2021). Populism in Place: The Economic Geography of the Globalization Backlash. *International Organization*, 75(2):464–494.

Brutger, R. and Guisinger, A. (2022). Labor Market Volatility, Gender, and Trade Preferences. *Journal of Experimental Political Science*, 9(2):189–202.

Brynjolfsson, E., Collis, A., and Eggers, F. (2019). Using Massive Online Choice Experiments to Measure Changes in Well-Being. *Proceedings of the National Academy of Sciences*, 116(15):7250–7255.

Brynjolfsson, E. and McAfee, A. (2014). *The Second Machine Age: Work, Progress, and Prosperity in a Time of Brilliant Technologies*. WW Norton.

Burman, A. and Sharma, U. (2021). *How Would Data Localization Benefit India?* Carnegie Endowment for International Peace.

Burri, M. and Polanco, R. (2020). Digital Trade Provisions in Preferential Trade Agreements: Introducing a New Dataset. *Journal of International Economic Law*, 23(1):187–220.

Büthe, T. and Mattli, W. (2011). *The New Global Rulers*. Princeton University Press.

Callander, S., Foarță, O. D., and Sugaya, T. (2021). *Market Competition and Political Influence: An Integrated Approach*. Centre for Economic Policy Research.

Casalini, F. and González, J. L. (2019). Trade and Cross-Border Data Flows. OECD Trade Policy Papers, No. 220. OECD Publishing.

Casalini, F., González, J. L., and Nemoto, T. (2021). Mapping Commonalities in Regulatory Approaches to Cross-Border Data Transfers. OECD Trade Policy Papers, No. 248, OECD Publishing.

Chander, A. (2013). *The Electronic Silk Road: How the Web Binds the World Together in Commerce*. Yale University Press.

Chander, A. (2019). The Internet of Things: Both Goods and Services. *World Trade Review*, 18(S1):S9–S22.

Chander, A. and Schwartz, P. M. (2022). Privacy and/or Trade. SSRN Scholarly Paper ID 4038531, Social Science Research Network.

Chander, A. and Sun, H. (2021). Sovereignty 2.0. SSRN Scholarly Paper ID 3904949, Social Science Research Network.

Chaudoin, S. and Mangini, M.-D. (2022). Robots, Foreigners, and Foreign Robots: Policy Responses to Automation and Trade. www.stephen chaudoin.com/chaudoin_mangini_automation.pdf.

Chazan, G. (2019). Angela Merkel urges EU to seize control of data from US tech titans. *Financial Times*. www.ft.com/content/956ccaa6-0537-11ea-9afa-d9e2401fa7ca.

Chen, C., Frey, C. B., and Presidente, G. (2022). Privacy Regulation and Firm Performance: Estimating the GDPR Effect Globally. No. 2022-1. The Oxford Martin Working Paper Series on Technological and Economic Change.

Chen, R. (2021). Mapping Data Governance Legal Frameworks Around the World: Findings from the Global Data Regulation Diagnostic. Policy Research Working Paper, No. 9615. World Bank. https://openknowledge .worldbank.org/handle/10986/35410.

Cheng, L., Liu, F., ad Yao, D. D. (2017). Enterprise Data Breach: Causes, Challenges, Prevention, and Future Directions. *WIREs Data Mining and Knowledge Discovery*, 7(5):e1211.

Colantone, I. and Stanig, P. (2018a). Global Competition and Brexit. *American Political Science Review*, 112(2):201–218.

Colantone, I. and Stanig, P. (2018b). The Trade Origins of Economic Nationalism: Import Competition and Voting Behavior in Western Europe. *American Journal of Political Science*, 62(4):936–953.

Commission, I. T. (2017). Global Digital Trade 1: Market Opportunities and Key Foreign Trade Restrictions. The U.S. International Trade Commission. www.usitc.gov/publications/industry_econ_analysis_332/2017/ global_digital_trade_1_market_opportunities_and.htm.

Cory, N. and Dascoli, L. (2021). How Barriers to Cross-Border Data Flows Are Spreading Globally, What They Cost, and How to Address Them. Information Technology and Innovation Foundation. https://itif.org/publicat ions/2021/07/19/how-barriers-cross-border-data-flows-are-spreading-glo bally-what-they-cost/.

Cowhey, P. F. and Aronson, J. D. (2017). *Digital DNA: Disruption and the Challenges for Global Governance*. Oxford University Press.

Culpepper, P. D. and Thelen, K. (2020). Are We All Amazon Primed? Consumers and the Politics of Platform Power. *Comparative Political Studies*, 53(2):288–318.

David, H. (2015). Why are there Still so Many Jobs? The History and Future of Workplace Automation. *Journal of Economic Perspectives*, 29(3):3–30.

Davis, C. L. (2004). International Institutions and Issue Linkage: Building Support for Agricultural Trade Liberalization. *American Political Science Review*, 98(1):153–169.

Davis, C. L. (2009). Overlapping Institutions in Trade Policy. *Perspectives on Politics*, 7(1):25–31.

Deardorff, A. (2017). Comparative Advantage in Digital Trade. In Evernett, S., editor, *Cloth for Wine? The Relevance of Ricardo's Comparative Advantage in the 21st Century*, 35–44. CEPR Press.

DeBrusk, C. (2018). The Risk of Machine-Learning Bias (and How to Prevent It). MIT Sloan Management Review. https://sloanreview.mit .edu/article/the-risk-of-machine-learning-bias-and-how-to-prevent-it/.

Deibert, R. and Rohozinski, R. (2010). Liberation vs. Control: The Future of Cyberspace. *Journal of Democracy*, 21(4):43–57.

Disdier, A.-C. and Head, K. (2008). The Puzzling Persistence of the Distance Effect on Bilateral Trade. *The Review of Economics and Statistics*, 90(1):37–48.

Djankov (2021). How Do Companies Avoid Paying International Taxes? PIIE. www.piie.com/sites/default/files/documents/djankov-international-tax-2021-09.pdf.

Dobbie, W., Liberman, A., Paravisini, D., and Pathania, V. (2018). Measuring Bias in Consumer Lending. Technical Report w24953, National Bureau of Economic Research.

Dorn, D., Hanson, G., and Majlesi, K. (2020). Importing Political Polarization? The Electoral Consequences of Rising Trade Exposure. *American Economic Review*, 110(10):3139–3183.

Dorn, D., Katz, L. F., Patterson, C., and Van Reenen, J. (2017). Concentrating on the Fall of the Labor Share. *American Economic Review*, 107(5): 180–185.

Dowd, R. (2022). Exporting the Digital Human Rights Norm. In Dowd, R., editor, *The Birth of Digital Human Rights: Digitized Data Governance as a Human Rights Issue in the EU*, Information Technology and Global Governance, pages 227–248. Springer.

Dragu, T. and Lupu, Y. (2021). Digital Authoritarianism and the Future of Human Rights. *International Organization*, 75(4):991–1017.

Eden, L., Srinivasan, N., and Lalapet, S. (2019). Transfer Pricing Challenges in the Digital Economy - Part 1: Hic Sunt Dracones? SSRN Scholarly Paper ID 3412546, Social Science Research Network.

Erie, M. S. and Streinz, T. (2021). The Beijing Effect: China's Digital Silk Road as Transnational Data Governance. *New York University Journal of International Law and Politics*, 54(1):1–92.

Fang, S. and Owen, E. (2011). International Institutions and Credible Commitment of Non-Democracies. *The Review of International Organizations*, 6(2):141–162.

Farrell, H. (2003). Constructing the International Foundations of E-Commerce—The EU-U.S. Safe Harbor Arrangement. *International Organization*, 57(2):277–306.

Farrell, H. and Newman, A. L. (2019a). *Of Privacy and Power*. Princeton University Press.

Farrell, H. and Newman, A. L. (2019b). Weaponized Interdependence: How Global Economic Networks Shape State Coercion. *International Security*, 44(1):42–79.

Ferencz, J. (2019). The OECD Digital Services Trade Restrictiveness Index. OECD Trade Policy Papers, No. 221, OECD Publishing. https://doi.org/10.1787/16ed2d78-en.

Ferracane, M. F. (2017). Restrictions on Cross-Border Data Flows: A Taxonomy. *SSRN Electronic Journal*. https://ecipe.org/publications/restrictions-to-cross-border-data-flows-a-taxonomy/.

Ferracane, M. F., Lee-Makiyama, H., and Van Der Marel, E. (2018). Digital Trade Restrictiveness Index. European Center for International Political Economy.

Ferracane, M. F. and van der Marel, E. (2021). *Regulating Personal Data: Data Models and Digital Services Trade*. Policy Research Working Papers. The World Bank.

Finnemore, M. and Sikkink, K. (1998). International Norm Dynamics and Political Change. *International Organization*, 52(4):887–917.

Frey, C. B. (2019). *The Technology Trap*. Princeton University Press.

Frey, C. B., Berger, T., and Chen, C. (2018). Political Machinery: Did Robots Swing the 2016 US Presidential Election? *Oxford Review of Economic Policy*, 34(3):418–442.

Frey, C. B. and Osborne, M. A. (2017). The Future of Employment: How Susceptible are Jobs to Computerisation? *Technological Forecasting and Social Change*, 114:254–280.

Frieden, J. A. and Rogowski, R. (1996). The Impact of the International Economy on National Policies: An Analytical Overview. *Internationalization and Domestic Politics*, 15:25–47.

Frier, S. (2018). Is Apple Really Your Privacy Hero? Bloomberg. August 8 https://www.bloomberg.com/news/articles/2018-08-08/is-apple-really-your-privacy-hero.

Furman, J., Coyle, D., Fletcher, A., McAuley, D., and Marsden, P. (2019). Unlocking Digital Competition: Report of the Digital Competition Expert Panel. UK Government Publication, HM Treasury.

Furman, J. and Orszag, P. (2018). A Firm-Level Perspective on the Role of Rents in the Rise in Inequality. In Martin Guzman, editor, *Toward a Just Society*, 19–47. Columbia University Press.

Gallego, A., Kuo, A., Manzano, D., and Fernández-Albertos, J. (2021). Technological Risk and Policy Preferences. *Comparative Political Studies*, 55(1): 60–92.

Gallego, A. and Kurer, T. (2022). Automation, Digitalization, and Artificial Intelligence in the Workplace: Implications for Political Behavior. *Annual Review of Political Science*, 25(1):null.

Gao, H. (2018). Digital or Trade? The Contrasting Approaches of China and US to Digital Trade. *Journal of International Economic Law*, 21(2):297–321.

Gereffi, G. and Fernandez-Stark, K. (2011). Global Value Chain Analysis: A Primer. Center on Globalization, Governance & Competitiveness (CGGC), Duke University.

Gidron, N. and Hall, P. A. (2017). The Politics of Social Status: Economic and Cultural Roots of the Populist Right. *The British Journal of Sociology*, 68: 57–84.

Gilardi, F. (2022). *Digital Technology, Politics, and Policy-Making*. Elements in Public Policy. Cambridge University Press.

Gingrich, J. (2019). Did State Responses to Automation Matter for Voters? *Research & Politics*, 6(1): 1–9.

Girard, T. (2022). National Identity, Public Opinion, and the Limits of Platform Power. Paper presented at the International Studies Association Annual Meeting.

Gohdes, A. R. (2014). Repression in the digital age: Communication technology and the politics of state violence. Doctoral dissertation, University of Mannheim. https://madoc.bib.uni-mannheim.de/37902.

Gohdes, A. R. (2020). Repression Technology: Internet Accessibility and State Violence. *American Journal of Political Science*, 64(3):488–503.

Goldfarb, A. and Tucker, C. (2019). Digital Economics. *Journal of Economic Literature*, 57(1):3–43.

Goldstein, J. L., Rivers, D., and Tomz, M. (2007). Institutions in International Relations: Understanding the Effects of the GATT and the WTO on World Trade. *International Organization*, 61(1):37–67.

Grossman, G. M. and Helpman, E. (1994). Protection for Sale. *The American Economic Review*, 84(4):833–850.

Grossman, G. M. and Rossi-Hansberg, E. (2008). Trading Tasks: A Simple Theory of Offshoring. *American Economic Review*, 98(5):1978–1997.

Guisinger, A. (2017). *American Opinion on Trade: Preferences without Politics*. Oxford University Press.

Gulotty, R. (2020). *Narrowing the Channel: The Politics of Regulatory Protection in International Trade*. University of Chicago Press.

Hai, Z. (2019). Automation and the Salience of Protectionism. Technical report, Working Paper. www.internationalpoliticaleconomysociety.org/sites/default/files/paper-uploads/2022-10-27-23_50_46-zuhadhai@stanford.edu.pdf.

Hainmueller, J. and Hiscox, M. J. (2006). Learning to Love Globalization: Education and Individual Attitudes Toward International Trade. *International Organization*, 60(2):469–498.

Hall, P. A. and Soskice, D. (2001). *Varieties of Capitalism: The Institutional Sources of Comparative Advantage*. Oxford University Press.

Handley, K. and Limão, N. (2015). Trade and Investment under Policy Uncertainty: Theory and Firm Evidence. *American Economic Journal: Economic Policy*, 7(4):189–222.

Handley, K. and Limão, N. (2017). Policy Uncertainty, Trade, and Welfare: Theory and Evidence for China and the United States. *American Economic Review*, 107(9):2731–2783.

Haskel, J. and Westlake, S. (2018). *Capitalism without Capital: The Rise of Intangible Economy*. Princeton University Press.

Hiscox, M. J. (2001). Class Versus Industry Cleavages: Inter-Industry Factor Mobility and the Politics of Trade. *International Organization*, 55(1):1–46.

Hodson, S. (2019). Applying WTO and FTA Disciplines to Data Localization Measures. *World Trade Review*, 18(4):579–607.

Hummels, D., Ishii, J., and Yi, K.-M. (2001). The Nature and Growth of Vertical Specialization in World Trade. *Journal of International Economics*, 54(1):75–96.

Hummels, D. L. and Schaur, G. (2013). Time as a Trade Barrier. *American Economic Review*, 103(7):2935–2959.

Iansiti, M. and Lakhani, K. R. (2020). *Competing in the Age of AI: Strategy and Leadership When Algorithms and Networks Run the World*. Harvard Business Press.

Im, Z. J., Mayer, N., Palier, B., and Rovny, J. (2019). The Losers of Automation: A Reservoir of Votes for the Radical Right? *Research & Politics*, 6(1): 1–7.

Iversen, T. and Soskice, D. (2019). *Democracy and Prosperity*. Princeton University Press.

Jardina, A. (2019). *White Identity Politics*. Cambridge University Press.

Jensen, J. B. (2011). *Global Trade in Services: Fear, Facts, and Offshoring*. Peterson Institute for International Economics.

Jensen, J. B., Quinn, D. P., and Weymouth, S. (2015). The Influence of Firm Global Supply Chains and Foreign Currency Undervaluations on US Trade Disputes. *International Organization*, 69(4): 913–947.

Jensen, J. B., Quinn, D. P., and Weymouth, S. (2017). Winners and Losers in International Trade: The Effects on US Presidential Voting. *International Organization*, 71(3):423–457.

Keck, M. E. and Sikkink, K. (2014). *Activists beyond Borders: Advocacy Networks in International Politics*. Cornell University Press.

Khan, L. (2018). The New Brandeis Movement: America's Antimonopoly Debate. *Journal of European Competition Law & Practice*, 9(3):131–132.

Kilic, B. and Avila, R. (2020). Cross Border Data Flows, Privacy, and Global Inequality. Public citizen. www.citizen.org/wp-content/uploads/crossborder-data-flows-privacy.pdf.

Kim, I. S. (2017). Political Cleavages within Industry: Firm-level Lobbying for Trade Liberalization. *The American Political Science Review*, 111(1):1.

Kim, I. S. and Milner, H. V. (2019). Multinational Corporations and their Influence Through Lobbying on Foreign Policy. In David Wessel, James Hines, and C. Fritz Foley editors, *Global Goliaths: Multinational Corporations in the 21st Century Economy*. Brookings Institution 497–536.

Kim, I. S. and Osgood, I. (2019). Firms in Trade and Trade Politics. *Annual Review of Political Science*, 22: 399–417.

King, G., Pan, J., and Roberts, M. E. (2013). How Censorship in China Allows Government Criticism but Silences Collective Expression. *American Political Science Review*, 107(2):326–343.

Korinek, A. and Stiglitz, J. E. (2019). *14. Artificial Intelligence and Its Implications for Income Distribution and Unemployment*. University of Chicago Press.

Koutroumpis, P., Leiponen, A., and Thomas, L. D. W. (2020). Markets for Data. *Industrial and Corporate Change*, 29(3):645–660.

Kröger, J. L., Miceli, M., and Müller, F. (2021). How Data Can Be Used Against People: A Classification of Personal Data Misuses. SSRN Scholarly Paper ID 3887097, Social Science Research Network.

Kurer, T. (2020). The Declining Middle: Occupational Change, Social Status, and the Populist Right. *Comparative Political Studies*, 53(10–11):1798–1835.

Kwet, M. (2019). Digital Colonialism: US Empire and the New Imperialism in the Global South. *Race & Class*, 60(4):3–26.

Lambrecht, A. and Tucker, C. (2019). Algorithmic Bias? An Empirical Study of Apparent Gender-based Discrimination in the Display of Stem Career Ads. *Management Science*, 65(7):2966–2981.

Lancieri, F. and Sakowski, P. M. (2021). Competition in Digital Markets: A Review of Expert Reports. *Stanford Journal of Law, Business and Finance*, 26:65.

Lehoucq, E. and Tarrow, S. (2020). The Rise of a Transnational Movement to Protect Privacy. *Mobilization: An International Quarterly*, 25(2):161–184.

Li, W. C. Y., Makoto, N., and Kazufumi, Y. (2019). *Value of Data: There's No Such Thing as a Free Lunch in the Digital Economy*. REITI

Liu, L. (2021). The Rise of Data Politics: Digital China and the World. *Studies in Comparative International Development*, 56(1):45–67.

Liu, L. (2022). *From Click to Boom: The Political Economy of E-Commerce in China*. Unpublished.

Lü, X., Scheve, K., and Slaughter, M. J. (2012). Inequity Aversion and the International Distribution of Trade Protection. *American Journal of Political Science*, 56(3):638–654.

Macher, J. T. and Mayo, J. W. (2015). Influencing Public Policymaking: Firm-, industry-, and Country-level Determinants. *Strategic Management Journal*, 36(13):2021–2038.

MacKinnon, R. (2012). Consent of the Networked: The Worldwide Struggle for Internet Freedom. *Politique étrangère*, 50(2):432–463.

Malhotra, N., Monin, B., and Tomz, M. (2019). Does Private Regulation Pre-empt Public Regulation? *American Political Science Review*, 113(1):19–37.

Mansfield, E. D., Milner, H. V., and Rudra, N. (2021). The Globalization Backlash: Exploring New Perspectives. *Comparative Political Studies*, 54(13):2267–2285.

Mansfield, E. D. and Mutz, D. C. (2009). Support for Free Trade: Self-Interest, Sociotropic Politics, and Out-Group Anxiety. *International Organization*, 63(3):425–457.

Mansfield, E. D. and Rudra, N. (2021). Embedded Liberalism in the Digital Era. *International Organization*, 75(2):558–585.

Manyika, J., Lund, S., Bughin, J. et al. (2016). *Digital Globalization: The New Era of Global Flows*. McKinsey Global Institute.

Mattoo, A. and Meltzer, J. P. (2018). International Data Flows and Privacy: The Conflict and Its Resolution. *Journal of International Economic Law*, 21(4):769–789.

Mayda, A. M. and Rodrik, D. (2005). Why are Some People (and Countries) More Protectionist than Others? *European Economic Review*, 49(6):1393–1430.

McAfee, A. and Brynjolfsson, E. (2017). *Machine, Platform, Crowd: Harnessing Our Digital Future*. WW Norton & Company.

Mele, C., Russo Spena, T., Kaartemo, V., and Marzullo, M. L. (2021). Smart Nudging: How Cognitive Technologies Enable Choice Architectures for Value Co-creation. *Journal of Business Research*.

Melitz, M. J. (2003). The Impact of Trade on Intra-industry Reallocations and Aggregate Industry Productivity. *Econometrica*, 71(6):1695–1725.

Meltzer, J. P. (2019). Governing Digital Trade. *World Trade Review*, 18(S1):S23–S48.

Milner, H. (1988). Trading Places: Industries for Free Trade. *World Politics*, 40(3):350–376.

Milner, H. V. (2021). Voting for Populism in Europe: Globalization, Technological Change, and the Extreme Right. *Comparative Political Studies*, 54(13):2286–2320.

Milner, H. V. and Kubota, K. (2005). Why the Move to Free Trade? Democracy and Trade Policy in the Developing Countries. *International Organization*, 59(1):107–143.

Moore, M. and Tambini, D. (2018). *Digital Dominance: The Power of Google, Amazon, Facebook, and Apple*. Oxford University Press.

Mutz, D. C. (2021). *Winners and Losers: The Psychology of Foreign Trade*, volume 27. Princeton University Press.

Mutz, D. C. and Kim, E. (2017). The Impact of In-group Favoritism on Trade Preferences. *International Organization*, 71(4):827–850.

Mutz, D. C. and Lee, A. H.-Y. (2020). How Much is One American Worth? How Competition Affects Trade Preferences. *American Political Science Review*, 114(4):1179–1194.

Nemoto, T. and Lopez Gonzalez, J. (2021). *Digital Trade Inventory: Rules, Standards and Principles*, OECD Trade Policy Papers, No. 251, OECD Publishing. https://doi.org/10.1787/9a9821e0-en.

Newman, A. L. (2008a). Building Transnational Civil Liberties: Transgovernmental Entrepreneurs and the European Data Privacy Directive. *International Organization*, 62(1):103–130.

Newman, A. L. (2008b). *Protectors of Privacy*. Cornell University Press.

Nguyen, D. and Paczos, M. (2020). *Measuring the Economic Value of Data and Cross-Border Data Flows: A Business Perspective*, OECD Digital Economy Papers, No. 297, OECD Publishing. https://doi.org/10.1787/6345995e-en.

OECD (2018). *Tax Challenges Arising from Digitalisation – Interim Report 2018: Inclusive Framework on BEPS*. OECD/G20 Base Erosion and Profit Shifting Project. OECD.

OECD (2019). *An Introduction to Online Platforms and Their Role in the Digital Transformation*. OECD.

Olson, M. (1965). *The Logic of Collective Action*. Harvard University Press.

Osgood, I. (2018). Globalizing the Supply Chain: Firm and Industrial Support for US Trade Agreements. *International Organization*, 72(2):455–484.

Osgood, I. (2021). Vanguards of Globalization: Organization and Political Action among America's Pro-trade Firms. *Business and Politics*, 23(1):1–35.

Osgood, I., Tingley, D., Bernauer, T. et al. (2017). The Charmed Life of Superstar Exporters: Survey Evidence on Firms and Trade Policy. *The Journal of Politics*, 79(1):133–152.

Owen, E. (2017). Exposure to Offshoring and the Politics of Trade Liberalization: Debate and Votes on Free Trade Agreements in the US House of Representatives, 2001–2006. *International Studies Quarterly*, 61(2):297–311.

Owen, E. and Walter, S. (2017). Open Economy Politics and Brexit: Insights, Puzzles, and Ways Forward. *Review of International Political Economy*, 24(2):179–202.

Peltzman, S. (1976). Toward a More General Theory of Regulation. *The Journal of Law and Economics*, 19(2):211–240.

Porter, M. E. (1985). Technology and Competitive Advantage. *Journal of Business Strategy*. 5(3):60–78.

Price, R. (1998). Reversing the Gun Sights: Transnational Civil Society Targets Land Mines. *International Organization*, 52(3):613–644.

Price, R. (2003). Transnational Civil Society and Advocacy in World Politics. *World Politics*, 55(4):579–606.

Raghavan, M., Barocas, S., Kleinberg, J., and Levy, K. (2020). Mitigating bias in algorithmic hiring: Evaluating claims and practices. In *Proceedings of the 2020 Conference on Fairness, Accountability, and Transparency*, pages 469–481.

Rho, S. and Tomz, M. (2017). Why don't trade preferences reflect economic self-interest? *International Organization*, 71(S1):S85–S108.

Richter, B. K., Samphantharak, K., and Timmons, J. F. (2009). Lobbying and taxes. *American Journal of Political Science*, 53(4):893–909.

Rickard, S. J. (2021). Incumbents Beware: The Impact of Offshoring on Elections. *British Journal of Political Science*, 52(2):758–780.

Risse, T., Risse-Kappen, T., Ropp, S. C., and Sikkink, K. (1999). *The Power of Human Rights: International Norms and Domestic Change*. Cambridge University Press.

Risse, T. and Sikkink, K. (1999). The Socialization of International Human Rights Norms into Domestic Practices: Introduction. In Thomas Risse, Stephen C. Ropp and Kathryn Sikkink, (eds.), *International Norms and Domestic Change*, Cambridge University Press. pp. 1–38.

Roberts, M. E. (2018). *Censored: Distraction and Diversion inside China's Great Firewall*. Princeton University Press.

Rodrik, D. (2011). *The Globalization Paradox: Why Global Markets, States, and Democracy Can't Coexist*. Oxford University Press.

Rogowski, R. (1987). Political Cleavages and Changing Exposure to Trade. *American Political Science Review*, 81(4): 1121–1137.

Rogowski, R. and Kayser, M. A. (2002). Majoritarian Electoral Systems and Consumer Power: Price-Level Evidence from the OECD Countries. *American Journal of Political Science*, 46(3):526–539.

Sandbu, M. (2019). More than Third of Foreign Investment is Multinationals Dodging Tax. *Financial Times*. www.ft.com/content/37aa9d06-d0c8-11e9-99a4-b5ded7a7fe3f.

Sarah, M. (2021). The role of online platforms in weathering the COVID-19 shock. OECD. www.oecd.org/coronavirus/policy-responses/the-role-of-online-platforms-in-weathering-the-covid-19-shock-2a3b8434/.

Scheve, K. F. and Slaughter, M. J. (2001). What Determines Individual Trade-policy Preferences? *Journal of International Economics*, 54(2):267–292.

Scholz, L. (2018). Big Data is Not Big Oil: The Role of Analogy in the Law of New Technologies. *SSRN Electronic Journal*.

Schulze, P. and van der Marel, E. (2021). Taxing digital services - compensating for the loss of competitiveness. Research Report 11/2021, ECIPE Policy Brief.

Sen, N. (2018). Understanding the Role of the WTO in International Data Flows: Taking the Liberalization or the Regulatory Autonomy Path? *Journal of International Economic Law*, 21(2):323–348.

Shapiro, C., Varian, H. R., and Carl, S. (1999). *Information Rules: A Strategic Guide to the Network Economy*. Harvard Business Press.

Sinha, A. and Basu, A. (2019). The Politics of India's Data Protection Ecosystem. *Economic and Political Weekly*, 54(49).

Slaughter, M. J. and McCormick, D. H. (2021). Data is Power: Washington Needs to Craft New Rules for the Digital Age. *Foreign Affairs* 100(3): 54.

Solove, D. J. (2021). The Myth of the Privacy Paradox. *George Washington Law Review*, 89:1.

Srivastava, S. (2021). Algorithmic Governance and the International Politics of Big Tech. *Perspectives on Politics*, 1–12.

Srivastava, S. (2022). *Hybrid Sovereignty in World Politics*. Cambridge University Press.

Stabell, C. B. and Fjeldstad, Ø. D. (1998). Configuring Value for Competitive Advantage: On Chains, Shops, and Networks. *Strategic Management Journal*, 19(5):413–437.

Stiglitz, J. (2019). *People, Power, and Profits: Progressive Capitalism for an Age of Discontent*. Penguin.

Stoller, M. (2019). *Goliath: The 100-Year War Between Monopoly Power and Democracy*. Simon & Schuster.

Strange, S. (1997). *Casino Capitalism*. Manchester University Press.

Subramanian, A. and Wei, S.-J. (2007). The WTO Promotes Trade, Strongly but Unevenly. *Journal of International Economics*, 72(1):151–175.

Susskind, J. (2022). *The Digital Republic: On Freedom and Democracy in the 21st Century*. Bloomsbury.

Teachout, Z. and Khan, L. M. (2014). Market Structure and Political Law: A Taxonomy of Power. *Duke Journal of Constitutional Law & Public Policy*, 9:37.

Thewissen, S. and Rueda, D. (2019). Automation and the Welfare State: Technological Change as a Determinant of Redistribution Preferences. *Comparative Political Studies*, 52(2):171–208.

Tørsløv, T. R., Wier, L. S., and Zucman, G. (2018). *The Missing Profits of Nations*. Technical report, National Bureau of Economic Research.

UNCTAD (2019). *Digital Economy Report 2019: Value Creation and Capture : Implications for Developing Countries*. United Nations Conference on Trade and Development.

UNCTAD (2021). *Digital Economy Report 2021: Cross-Border Data Flows and Development : From Whom the Data Flow*. United Nations Conference on Trade and Development.

Véliz, C. (2020). *Privacy Is Power*. Random House Australia.

Walter, S. (2017). Globalization and the Demand-Side of Politics: How Globalization Shapes Labor Market Risk Perceptions and Policy Preferences*. *Political Science Research and Methods*, 5(1):55–80.

Walter, S. (2021). The Backlash Against Globalization. *Annual Review of Political Science*, 24(1):421–442.

Wasik, B. (2015). Welcome to the Age of Digital Imperialism. *The New York Times*. www.nytimes.com/2015/06/07/magazine/welcome-to-the-age-of-digital-imperialism.html.

Weiss, J. C. (2019). A World Safe for Autocracy: China's Rise and the Future of Global Politics Essays. *Foreign Affairs*, 98(4):92–108.

Weiss, J. C. and Wallace, J. L. (2021). Domestic Politics, China's Rise, and the Future of the Liberal International Order. *International Organization*, 75(2):635–664.

Weymouth, S. (2012). Firm Lobbying and Influence in Developing Countries: A Multilevel Approach. *Business and Politics*, 14(4):1–26.

Weymouth, S. (2016). Competition Politics: Interest Groups, Democracy, and Antitrust Reform in Developing Countries. *The Antitrust Bulletin*, 61(2):296–316.

Weymouth, S. (2017). Service Firms in the Politics of US Trade Policy. *International Studies Quarterly*, 61(4):935–947.

World Bank, editor (2021). *World Development Report 2021: Data for Better Lives*. World Development Report. World Bank.

WTO (2016). World Trade Report 2016: Levelling the Trading Field for SMEs. WTO.

Wu, M. (2016). The China, Inc. Challenge to Global trade governance. *Harv. Int'l LJ*, 57:261.

Wu, M. (2017). Digital Trade-Related Provisions in Regional Trade Agreements: Existing Models and Lessons for the Multilateral Trade System. RTA Exchange. *International Centre for Trade and Sustainable Development (ICTSD) and the Inter-American Development Bank, Geneva, Switzerland. using blockchain to facilitate trade for sd*, 269.

Wu, M. (2019). 11 China's Rise and the Growing Doubts over Trade Multilateralism. In Meredith A. Crowley, editor, *Trade War: The Clash of Economic Systems Threatening Global Prosperity*, 101–110. CEPR Press.

Wu, N. (2021). Misattributed Blame? Attitudes toward Globalization in the Age of Automation. *Political Science Research and Methods*, 10(3): 1–18.

Wu, T. (2020). *The Curse of Bigness: How Corporate Giants Came to Rule the World*. Atlantic Books.

Young, A. (2022). Wrestling Referees?: The EU's Place in Governing the Global Digital Economy. Working paper presented at the International Studies Association Annual Meeting.

Zhang, D. and Kong, Q. (2021). How Does Energy Policy Affect Firms' Outward Foreign Direct Investment: An Explanation Based on Investment Motivation and Firms' Performance. *Energy Policy*, 158:112548.

Zingales, L. (2017). Towards a Political Theory of the Firm. *Journal of Economic Perspectives*, 31(3):113–130.

Zuboff, S. (2019). *The Age of Surveillance Capitalism: The Fight for a Human Future at the New Frontier of Power*. Profile Books.

Zucman, G. (2015). *The Hidden Wealth of Nations: The Scourge of Tax Havens*. University of Chicago Press.

Cambridge Elements ☰

International Relations

Series Editors

Jon C. W. Pevehouse
University of Wisconsin–Madison

Jon C. W. Pevehouse is the Vilas Distinguished Achievement Professor of Political Science at the University of Wisconsin–Madison. He has published numerous books and articles in IR in the fields of international political economy, international organizations, foreign policy analysis, and political methodology. He is a former editor of the leading IR field journal, International Organization.

Tanja A. Börzel
Freie Universität Berlin

Tanja A. Börzel is the Professor of political science and holds the Chair for European Integration at the Otto-Suhr-Institute for Political Science, Freie Universität Berlin. She holds a PhD from the European University Institute, Florence, Italy. She is coordinator of the Research College "The Transformative Power of Europe," as well as the FP7-Collaborative Project "Maximizing the Enlargement Capacity of the European Union" and the H2020 Collaborative Project "The EU and Eastern Partnership Countries: An Inside-Out Analysis and Strategic Assessment." She directs the Jean Monnet Center of Excellence "Europe and its Citizens."

Edward D. Mansfield
University of Pennsylvania

Edward D. Mansfield is the Hum Rosen Professor of Political Science, University of Pennsylvania. He has published well over 100 books and articles in the area of international political economy, international security, and international organizations. He is Director of the Christopher H. Browne Center for International Politics at the University of Pennsylvania and former program co-chair of the American Political Science Association.

Editorial Team

International Relations Theory
Jeffrey T. Checkel, European University Institute, Florence
Miles Kahler, American University Washington, D.C.

International Security
Sarah Kreps, Cornell University
Anna Leander, Graduate Institute Geneva

International Political Economy
Edward D. Mansfield, University of Pennsylvania
Stafanie Walter, University of Zurich

International Organisations
Tanja A. Börzel, Freie Universität Berlin
Jon C. W. Pevehouse, University of Wisconsin–Madison

About the Series

The Cambridge Elements Series in International Relations publishes original research on key topics in the field. The series includes manuscripts addressing international security, international political economy, international organizations, and international relations.

Cambridge Elements ≡

International Relations

Elements in the Series

A full series listing is available at: www.cambridge.org/EIR

Printed in the United States
by Baker & Taylor Publisher Services